ESSENTIAL HISTORIES

The Northern Ireland Troubles 1969–2007

Aaron Edwards

OSPREY PUBLISHING
Bloomsbury Publishing Plc
Kemp House, Chawley Park, Cumnor Hill, Oxford OX2 9PH, UK
29 Earlsfort Terrace, Dublin 2, Ireland
1385 Broadway, 5th Floor, New York, NY 10018, USA
E-mail: info@ospreypublishing.com
www.ospreypublishing.com

OSPREY is a trademark of Osprey Publishing Ltd

First published in Great Britain in 2023

The text in this edition is revised and updated from: ESS 73: *The Northern Ireland Troubles: Operation Banner 1969–2007* (Osprey Publishing, 2011).

Essential Histories Series Editor: Professor Robert O'Neill

A catalogue record for this book is available from the British Library.

ISBN: PB 9781472857149;
eBook 9781472857170;
ePDF 9781472857163;
XML 9781472857187

23 24 25 26 27   10 9 8 7 6 5 4 3 2 1

Cover design by Stewart Larking
Maps and diagram by Peter Bull, revised by J B Illustrations.
Maps on pages 36 and 97 further revised by www.bounford.com
Index by Alison Worthington
Typeset by PDQ Digital Media Solutions, Bungay, UK
Printed and bound in India by Replika Press Private Ltd.

Osprey Publishing supports the Woodland Trust, the UK's leading woodland conservation charity.

To find out more about our authors and books visit www.ospreypublishing.com. Here you will find extracts, author interviews, details of forthcoming events and the option to sign up for our newsletter.

CONTENTS

INTRODUCTION

For more than a generation Northern Ireland was the site of one of Europe's bloodiest and most protracted conflicts. Between 1969 and 2007 the 'Troubles', as the conflict became euphemistically known, claimed the lives of around 3,700 people, with over ten times as many injured in countless bomb and gun attacks. The armed conflict was primarily fought between Protestant unionists who wished to retain their connection with Great Britain under the Act of Union of 1800 and Catholic nationalists who wished to break the link and forge an independent sovereign country. Tit-for-tat killings between those more extreme Protestants, known as loyalists, and their Catholic counterparts, known as republicans, became commonplace. These sectarian assassinations entrenched the bitterness and hatred that continues to polarize relations between and within communities in Northern Ireland today. But what are the origins of the Troubles? How did the main protagonists fight their 'war'? And why did political violence persist for so long? Moreover, what lessons can be drawn from the transition from the long war to a long peace?

Although the conflict between unionists and nationalists has its roots in the settler–native confrontations of the 17th century, its most recent phase can be traced to the partition of Ireland and the formation of a separate devolved administration for Northern Ireland in the 1920s, and the subsequent hold over politics, culture and society enjoyed by the Ulster Unionist Party until the collapse of that administration in March 1972. In the late 1960s nationalists, republicans and socialists – along with a handful of Protestants – opposed to the unionist dominance of political life founded the Northern Ireland Civil Rights Association (NICRA). The organization aimed 'to bring to Northern Ireland effective democracy, and to end all the forms of

OPPOSITE
The 1st Dragoons and 78th Highlanders scatter Catholic and Protestant rioters in Belfast in August 1872. One contemporary newspaper reported 'desperate scenes of bloodshed and strife'. (Photo by Culture Club/ Bridgeman via Getty Images)

Students from Queen's University Belfast on a protest march in October 1968. The Northern Ireland civil rights movement called for an end to discrimination in jobs, housing and votes. (© IWM HU 55866)

injustice, intimidation, discrimination and deprivation, which result from the partisan rule of the Stormont regime'. Many activists were exercised by what they saw as the local unionist regime's discriminatory policies towards them in employment, housing and electoral politics, while a minority of extremists were intent on sparking civil unrest and anarchy. The storm whipped up by NICRA protest marches would lead to a groundswell of support for a radical redistribution of these civil rights, eventually bringing both communities into direct confrontation with one another.

The NICRA marches sparked off counter-demonstrations led by the fundamentalist Protestant preacher Reverend Ian Paisley, whose oratory sent crowds into frenzied hysteria when civil rights marches passed through predominantly unionist areas. Heavy-handed responses by militant loyalists and elements of the local Royal Ulster Constabulary (RUC) and its auxiliary Ulster Special Constabulary (USC, or 'B' Specials) provoked

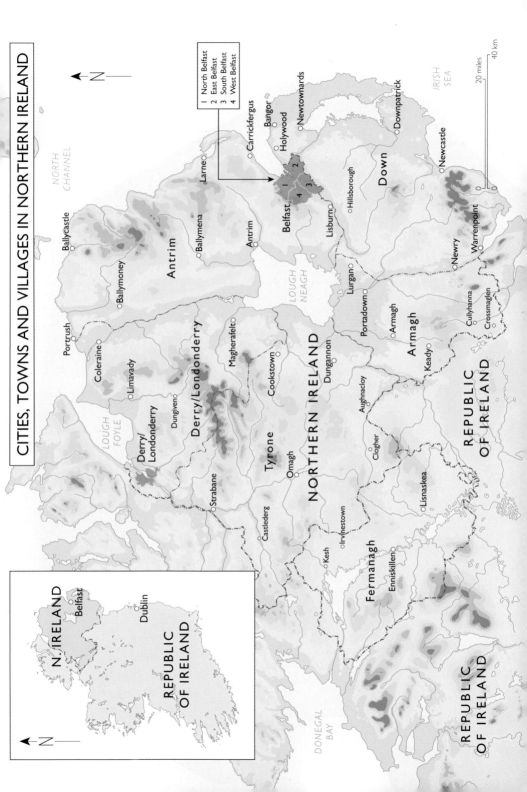

CITIES, TOWNS AND VILLAGES IN NORTHERN IRELAND

1 North Belfast
2 East Belfast
3 South Belfast
4 West Belfast

NORTH CHANNEL

IRISH SEA

N

Ballycastle
Portrush
Ballymoney
Coleraine
Limavady
Dungiven
Derry/Londonderry
LOUGH FOYLE
Strabane
Castlederg
Kesh
Irvinestown
Enniskillen
Lisnaskea
Fermanagh
Clogher
Aughnacloy
Omagh
Tyrone
Cookstown
Magherafelt
Ballymena
Antrim
Antrim
Larne
Carrickfergus
Bangor
Holywood
Newtownards
Belfast
Lisburn
Hillsborough
Down
Downpatrick
Newcastle
LOUGH NEAGH
Dungannon
Lurgan
Portadown
Armagh
Armagh
Keady
Newry
Warrenpoint
Cullyhanna
Crossmaglen

NORTHERN IRELAND

REPUBLIC OF IRELAND

REPUBLIC OF IRELAND

20 miles
40 km

N

N. IRELAND
Belfast

Dublin

REPUBLIC OF IRELAND

DONEGAL BAY

The RUC requested the support of the British Army initially in Derry/Londonderry on 14 August 1969. Soldiers were last deployed on the streets during the IRA border campaign of 1956–62. (Photo by Peter Ferraz/Getty Images)

further unrest and violence. The reformist impulse behind the initial civil rights marches soon gave way to a mushrooming of militancy. Protestants were jettisoned from NICRA's ranks, and the province spiralled further into sectarian clashes and civil disorder.

In the heightened atmosphere of the Orange Order's annual marching season during the summer of 1969,

nationalist protestors soon found themselves in open conflict with their unionist neighbours and the police. Widespread sectarian rioting led to the formation of vigilante groups as respective communities clashed on the streets of Northern Ireland. The Troubles, which had lain subdued since the 1920s – with only the occasional glimmer of violence – had been reignited.

In what one local newspaper declared 'an orgy of violence', mobs attacked RUC officers and police stations in the cities of Belfast and Londonderry and in the rural towns of Crossmaglen, Newry, Coalisland and Dungannon. As violence escalated, the Irish Republican Army (IRA), an organization formed during the Irish revolutionary period half a century earlier – and since driven underground – emerged to defend the beleaguered nationalist community. The battle lines were now drawn for an armed conflict between the RUC, Army and IRA.

Few actions in the Troubles were as momentous as the intervention of British troops. Ordered onto the province's streets on 14 August 1969 by Home Secretary James Callaghan, following a request by his counterpart in the Northern Ireland government, the troops' task was to 'provide military assistance to the civil power'. Despite its initial peacekeeping posture, the British Army was very quickly thrust into the midst of a vicious cycle of violence within a divided community. Between 1971 and 1997 Britain saw approximately 744 members of its armed forces personnel killed in hostilities and countless others wounded. Approximately 250,000 soldiers qualified for the Northern Ireland clasp of the Army's General Service Medal, with Operation *Banner* becoming the longest military campaign in modern British history.

Operation *Banner* lasted longer than the Palestine deployment under the British Mandate (1920s to the 1940s) and was infinitely more complex and controversial than the short-lived Aden campaign of the 1960s. Politically, many high-profile atrocities – such as the indiscriminate bombing of civilian targets by the various terrorist groups – provoked universal outrage. The sometimes knee-jerk reactions of the Security Forces – made up of the RUC, the locally recruited Ulster Defence Regiment (UDR, later the Royal Irish Regiment Home Service Force), and the British Army – from time to time also served to generate international furore and led to high-profile inquiries. The Parker and

Compton Inquiries investigated allegations of the ill-treatment of terrorist suspects, while the Saville Inquiry was appointed to determine responsibility for the events of 'Bloody Sunday', when soldiers shot dead 14 people. These investigations portrayed Britain and its Security Forces in a poor light and, arguably, handed propaganda victories to militant republicans.

Many nationalists joined the IRA, a clandestine organization with a long lineage stretching back to the separatist Fenian Movement and the Irish Republican Brotherhood. In 25 years of violence, republican paramilitaries (mainly the IRA) were responsible for the murders of over 2,000 people – mostly Protestants. Loyalist paramilitary organizations – some formed in anticipation of the escalation of republican violence and others as vigilante defence groups – killed over 1,018 people, mostly Catholics. The Security Forces were responsible for approximately 363 deaths. Despite the highly sophisticated propaganda campaigns undertaken by terrorists, the sad truth was that most victims of the Troubles were Protestant and Catholic civilians. Even with the running-down of their respective military campaigns and the onset of the 'peace process' in the 1990s, paramilitaries continued to harass their respective communities with intimidation, threats, violence and murder.

While the 1998 Belfast (or 'Good Friday') Agreement saw the main unionist and nationalist traditions reach a political accommodation, violence continued on the streets until the decommissioning of IRA weapons in 2005. The British Army was finally withdrawn from the streets and Operation *Banner* terminated in July 2007. Power-sharing institutions were finally devolved by the British government to the local Stormont Assembly in a deal between Ian Paisley's Democratic Unionist Party (DUP) and Gerry Adams' Sinn Féin in May 2007. Loyalist paramilitaries finally ended their own terror campaigns in 2009. All these developments helped stabilize the fledgling peace process in the decade after the signing of the Belfast Agreement.

BACKGROUND TO WAR
Politics and violence

In Ireland, history weighs heavily on the minds of the people. Although admittedly something of a cliché, it is undeniable that there is a predilection for the Irish to remember the far-distant past as strongly as more recent events. And like all monochrome remembrances of the past, there has also been a tendency towards the deeply selective. When viewed through the prism of perceived oppression, sacrifice and injustice, these deep-rooted interpretations of the past have led to embittered feelings towards 'the other side'. The myths, memories and symbols of Irish nationalism and Ulster unionism are self-perpetuating narratives that have served to reinforce the divisions between these two main communities in Northern Ireland. And it is the polarizing effect that this has had that has made the Troubles so enduring.

Conventional wisdom would have us believe that the conflict in Ireland can be distilled into a virulent antagonism between the Irish and the English, but this only masks a deeper-rooted truth that Irish people are – first and foremost – divided among themselves. In the words of Nobel Peace Prize winner and former Social Democratic and Labour Party (SDLP) politician John Hume, '[t]wo major political traditions share the island of Ireland. We are destined by history to live side by side.' The two principal political traditions inhabit 'two lands on one soil', but the longevity of the most recent violent phase of the Northern Ireland conflict indicates how strongly they disagree with one another over the design of the constitutional architecture to be built there.

A towering nationalist figure, Hume realized that there was more to it than the crude republican mantra of 'eight centuries of English subjugation of Ireland'. In the late 1980s and early 1990s Hume embarked on a dialogue to persuade Gerry Adams, the leader of the IRA's political associates in Sinn Féin, and other militant republicans to rethink their dogmatic views on the role of the British government and the position of the unionist community in Ireland. Ironically, Sinn Féin would eventually overtake Hume's SDLP at the polls in the wake of the signing of the Belfast Agreement in 1998 to become the largest nationalist party in Northern Ireland.

Introducing the gun into Irish politics

Advances in historical scholarship over the years have ensured a more sober analysis of the role of the British government in Ireland, hinting at its steady process of disengagement since before World War I. This has not always been welcome, with unionists resisting any attempts to force Home Rule upon them, while nationalists have attempted to hasten Britain's total disengagement. In 'Ulster's Solemn League and Covenant' of 1912, 237,368 men and 234,046 women pledged themselves

> … in solemn Covenant, throughout this our time of threatened calamity to stand by one another in defending for ourselves and our children our cherished position of equal citizenship in the United Kingdom and in using all means which may be found necessary to defeat the present conspiracy to set up a Home Rule Parliament in Ireland.

The resolve of unionists to oppose unpopular British policy in Ireland by signing up to the Covenant marked them out as 'Queen's rebels', meaning they were prepared to accept British rule from London but not when it ran contrary to the unionist community's interests in Ulster. Contrary to the Irish republican claim that unionists are 'misguided Irishmen', they have proved resilient in maintaining the link with Great Britain for myriad political, social and economic reasons.

Nevertheless, four years into the Third Home Rule Crisis (1910–14), unionists were on the back foot. Home Rule looked inevitable. Unionists responded by drilling, first with dummy rifles, and then with thousands of Mannlicher M1904 and Mauser Gew 88 rifles from Germany, and an assortment of pistols landed illegally at the ports of Larne and Donaghadee. They established a paramilitary Ulster Volunteer Force (UVF) commanded by seasoned members of the British officer corps along with a cadre of Army NCOs. A tense situation developed. Feeling themselves to be under threat too, nationalists formed their own militias, thus preparing the path towards civil war. Unionists accused the British government of betrayal, a mood captured eloquently by Rudyard Kipling in his poem *Ulster 1912*:

> The blood our fathers spilt,
> Our love, our toils, our pains
> Are counted us for guilt
> And only bind our chains –
> Before an Empire's eyes
> The traitor claims his price.
> What need of further lies?
> We are the sacrifice.

Meanwhile, events beyond Ireland's shores intervened. The assassination of the Archduke Franz Ferdinand by Young Bosnia member Gavrilo Princip in Sarajevo triggered a series of events that would draw Britain into World War I. Irishmen promptly answered the call, serving in their hundreds of thousands, mainly along the Western Front. Local disputes were suspended in favour of what nationalist leader John Redmond called

the 'two-fold duty' of all Irishmen – to soldier 'wherever the firing line extends in defence of the right of freedom and religion in this war'.

With the onset of the Anglo-Irish War of Independence of 1919–21, London acted as a constitutional midwife, helping to deliver self-government for North and South by passing the Government of Ireland Act in 1920. It was this legislation that formally partitioned the six north-eastern counties of the ancient nine-county province of Ulster from the 26 south-western counties of Ireland's other three provinces of Leinster, Munster and Connaught. Although Ireland had fallen under English influence from the 12th century onwards, it had only officially been part of the United Kingdom since the Act of Union came into effect in 1801. The Government of Ireland Act established two separate parliaments in Belfast and Dublin, though London

Sir Edward Carson (1854–1935) was the founder of the paramilitary Ulster Volunteer Force. Born in Dublin, he would become the most revered of Ulster Unionist leaders. (Photo by Spencer Arnold Collection/Hulton Archive/Getty Images)

A riot in York Street in 1920. Located near Belfast Docks, this area was the scene of sectarian tensions between Protestant unionists and Catholic nationalists in Northern Ireland's early years. (Photo © Hulton-Deutsch Collection/CORBIS/ Corbis via Getty Images)

held a firm grip on reserved matters like foreign policy, currency, taxation and access to ports in both jurisdictions. It was envisaged that Ireland would eventually be reunited within the framework of the United Kingdom.

The reunification of Ireland proved impossible for a variety of reasons, not least because of the entrenched position adopted by Ulster Unionists, who were reluctant to countenance any further secession from the UK. Instead, following the ceasefire between the British Army and the IRA in 1921, the signing of the Anglo-Irish Treaty established the southern 26 counties as the Irish Free State (Eire), with Dominion status. Northern Ireland rejected rule from Dublin. The unionists were also worried about the incursion of IRA 'flying columns' north of the border; the threat of a hostile neighbouring state sponsoring guerrilla forces loomed large in unionist minds. This existential fear led to the establishment of an internal security apparatus, incorporating the Ulster Special Constabulary in 1920 and the Royal Ulster Constabulary in 1922. The process of state formation, however, was an uphill struggle that took place against the backdrop of violence on the streets. Between 1920 and 1922 approximately 491 people lost their lives; a similar number would die 50 years later in 1972, the single worst year of the more recent Troubles.

The birth of Northern Ireland

The new political entity of Northern Ireland was born out of conflict, as the project of Home Rule for Ireland floundered amid the staunch opposition of Ulster Unionists. Matters were not helped much by the southern state, which under President Éamon de Valera's watchful eye sought to integrate Church and State more closely together into a single nationalist regime in Dublin. De Valera's own staunch Roman Catholicism left him determined to govern according to exclusively Gaelic traditions. These were absolutely alien to Protestant unionists, who looked towards the more secular and progressive basis of their union with Great Britain.

Table 1. Prime Ministers of Northern Ireland, 1921–72		
Prime Minister	**Entered Office**	**Left Office**
James Craig	7 June 1921	24 November 1940
John Miller Andrews	27 November 1940	1 May 1943
Basil Brooke	1 May 1943	25 March 1963
Terence O'Neill	25 March 1963	1 May 1969
James Chichester-Clark	1 May 1969	23 March 1971
Brian Faulkner	23 March 1971	30 March 1972

Sir James Craig (1871–1940), Northern Ireland's first prime minister (centre, seated), with his cabinet in the 1920s. Also pictured (top right) is senior official Sir Ernest Clark, who helped establish Northern Ireland. (Photo by George Rinhart/Corbis via Getty Images)

Such was the determination to resist incorporation into the southern state that the unionist administration began to equate its own dominance over local politics, society and culture with the survival of Northern Ireland itself. The Orange Order, an oath-bound society formed in the aftermath of a sectarian skirmish in the late 18th century, was used as the adhesive to bind together an uneasy class alliance, and it became the cushion upon which unionist control and authority rested. When de Valera declared Eire to be 'a Catholic state for Catholic people', Sir James Craig (later Lord Craigavon), Northern Ireland's first prime minister, responded with the (often misquoted) adage about Northern Ireland having 'a Protestant people and a Protestant parliament'. An air of suspicion descended over both parts of the island, marginalizing any popular desire in both jurisdictions for reunification.

Despite building its government around the philosophy of including loyalists while excluding what unionist leaders called 'disloyalists', the regime was divided over the best way to maintain Northern Ireland's status within the United Kingdom. Other unionists, such as the head of the Northern Ireland civil service, Sir Wilfred Spender, preferred a more inclusive agenda that reflected political practices in Great Britain. As a by-product of this sectional agenda Catholics played little active role in politics.

This disgruntlement extended to Craig's own support base, particularly amongst the working class who, by the Second World War, were involved in large-scale industrial unrest which gave the impression that Northern Ireland was only 'half in the war'. The growing militancy amongst workers eventually led to the downfall of Craig's successor, John Miller Andrews, and his replacement by Sir Basil Brooke, the nephew of Viscount Alanbrooke, the Chief of the Imperial General Staff. Brooke had served as a cabinet minister under Craig and Andrews. As a supporter of Craig's narrow agenda he reluctantly agreed to adopt new social welfare legislation at Westminster in a bid to placate the working classes. Although the growing political threat posed by the labour movement in Northern Ireland was halted in the 1945 elections, Brooke instinctively knew he would have to do more to maintain the union.

In 1948 Irish Taoiseach John A. Costello declared his intent to lead the Free State out of the Commonwealth and towards becoming an independent republic. This in turn provoked extensive lobbying by Basil Brooke on behalf of his government. Brooke's unflinching commitment to the Union, not to mention his obvious diplomatic skills and charm, ensured that he won the support of British Prime Minister Clement Attlee. Britain's Labour government passed the Ireland Act in 1949, which gave an undertaking that Northern Ireland would not cease to be part of the United Kingdom 'without the consent of the Parliament of Northern Ireland'.

The IRA posed a persistent threat to Northern Ireland, prosecuting a border offensive in 1956–62. Here a captured IRA member is questioned by the RUC in Lisnaskea, County Fermanagh. (Photo by Charles Hewitt/Picture Post/Hulton Archive/Getty Images)

The border campaign: Operation *Harvest*

Despite the Ireland act cementing Northern Ireland's place in the Union with Great Britain, challenges still remained. The IRA had been a constant threat to the Unionist regime throughout its 50 years of existence. Between 1956 and 1962 it prosecuted a violent campaign – codenamed Operation *Harvest* – against the Northern Ireland state, attacking infrastructure targets, such as bridges and the sole BBC transmitter in the province, in a half-hearted bid to end partition. The campaign failed for a number of reasons, including a lack of tactical experience amongst its commanders, the difficulty of connecting these to a realistic strategy and, perhaps most importantly, the lack of widespread support from the Catholic minority.

Speaking in the Stormont Parliament on 18 December 1956, a week after the IRA declared its 'people in the Six

Counties have taken the fight to the enemy', the Minister for Home Affairs W. B. Topping said:

> Every bullet fired, every bomb thrown, every act of violence which takes place only hammers another nail in the coffin of Republican hopes. It is astonishing that those who are responsible for these acts of violence have not yet learned that bullets cannot shoot beliefs. We believe in Britain and in the British way of life. We are British and British we will remain. (Hon. Members: Hear, hear.)

Security briefings to the Stormont government at the time spoke in terms of the calmness displayed by both communities and sharply contrasted this round of violence with that experienced in the 1920s. Within a year the RUC was reporting how 'the life of the community remains largely unaffected'. Several top-level police reports commended Brooke and his colleagues for consistently urging restraint among their supporters.

Table 2. Presidents of the Executive and Taoisigh of the Republic of Ireland		
President of the Executive	**Entered office**	**Left office**
William T. Cosgrave	6 December 1922	9 March 1932
Éamon de Valera	9 March 1932	29 December 1937
Taoiseach	**Entered office**	**Left office**
Éamon de Valera	29 December 1937	18 February 1948
John A. Costello	18 February 1948	13 June 1951
Éamon de Valera	13 June 1951	2 June 1954
John A. Costello	2 June 1954	20 March 1957
Éamon de Valera	20 March 1957	23 June 1959
Seán Lemass	23 June 1959	10 November 1966
Jack Lynch	10 November 1966	14 March 1973

Liam Cosgrove	14 March 1973	5 July 1977
Jack Lynch	5 July 1977	11 December 1979
Charles J. Haughey	11 December 1979	30 June 1981
Garret FitzGerald	30 June 1981	9 March 1982
Charles J. Haughey	9 March 1982	14 December 1982
Garret FitzGerald	14 December 1982	10 March 1987
Charles J. Haughey	10 March 1987	11 February 1992
Albert Reynolds	11 February 1992	15 December 1994
John Bruton	15 December 1994	26 June 1997
Bertie Ahern	26 June 1997	7 May 2008
Brian Cowen	7 May 2008	9 March 2011
Enda Kenny	9 March 2011	14 June 2017
Leo Varadkar	14 June 2017	27 June 2020
Micheál Martin	27 June 2020	17 December 2022
Leo Varadkar	17 December 2022	Incumbent

In any case the IRA's objectives were unrealistic given the detachment of many nationalists from the political process. Following the resounding failure of the Anti-Partition League earlier in the decade to achieve the abolition of the border in a peaceful manner, constitutional nationalism was quickly supplanted by a more militant republicanism. An IRA statement released after the first wave of attacks stated:

Out of this national liberation struggle a new Ireland will emerge, upright and free. In that new Ireland we shall build a country fit for all our people to live in. That then is our aim: an independent, united, democratic Irish Republic. For this we shall fight until the invader is driven from our soil and victory is ours.

By launching pre-planned attacks on military and infrastructure targets dotted along the border of

Northern Ireland from the 'safe haven' of the Irish Republic, the IRA sought to end partition by physical force. Most commentators writing about this period in Northern Ireland's history tend to dismiss the IRA's border campaign as insignificant, mainly because of the small number of fatalities involved. In total 16 people lost their lives – ten IRA men and six policemen – and scores were wounded. In light of what was to emerge by the end of the 1960s this is certainly a superficially attractive observation. However, it somewhat misses the point that the Unionist government was under immense pressure from its grassroots to act against the terrorists.

In a speech at Stormont on 4 July 1957, the same day that an RUC constable was murdered and his colleague seriously injured in an IRA ambush, Unionist MP for Antrim Nat Minford led calls for tougher security measures:

The IRA's border campaign was a failure. However, as this picture shows, the organization plotted a new offensive to coincide with the 50th anniversary of the Easter Rising in 1966. (Photo by Terence Spencer/ Popperfoto via Getty Images)

The laws that have been in operation in Cyprus should be enforced here. A man who carries a gun or in any way assists another to carry a gun is not out for the good of the public, and the only punishment should be death.*

Although the use of the death penalty was not seriously entertained, the Unionist authorities did turn to tougher measures, under the provisions of the Special Powers Act of 1922. Internment was introduced for the first time in Northern Ireland. The coercive nature of the Unionist response was dictated primarily by the need to prevent anger among grassroots unionists from boiling over into reprisals. Not for the first time would the Unionist government act to counter angst and threats of vigilantism from among its supporters. The Brooke administration's actions were soon complemented by de Valera, whose administration interned IRA suspects south of the border in a bid to offset pressure from London. Within a year 500 suspects had been interned on both sides of the border. Over the next few years the IRA's violence became more sporadic until it fizzled out and the organization called a halt to its armed campaign in February 1962.

The resurgence of loyalist extremism and vigilantism

Violence once again returned to Northern Ireland's streets in 1964. This time it was caused by the presence of an Irish tricolour in the window of a shop being used as a headquarters by William 'Billy' McMillen, who was contesting the Westminster seat of West Belfast. Fundamentalist Protestant preacher Ian Paisley led a mob into Divis Street, West Belfast, to remove the flag. Three nights of serious rioting gripped Belfast and the RUC

---

*   A major counter-insurgency campaign was fought by Britain's Security Forces in Cyprus between 1955 and 1959. The Greek terrorist group EOKA, led by the ex-Greek Army colonel George Grivas, embarked on a campaign of subversion known as *enosis*, which aimed to reunite the island by force of arms.

deployed water cannon to quell the disturbances. Scores of Catholic youths later arrested remarked in court that they would not have taken to the streets had it not been for Paisley's intervention.

Anticipating a further upsurge in IRA activity, some right-wing unionist politicians resurrected the UVF in late 1965 as a means of marshalling vigilante spirit among sections of the Protestant working class. The UVF was a tiny but deadly organization, born out of political intrigue and incubated in the shadows of a Unionist establishment worried about the liberal-leaning policies of Terence O'Neill, Northern Ireland's modernizing fourth prime minister. O'Neill had promised to 'transform the face of Ulster' but he fatally misunderstood the dynamics of sectarianism. Clandestine bomb attacks carried out by the UVF, and subsequently blamed on the IRA, were used as an instrument to force O'Neill's hand towards more coercive anti-IRA measures. Such scare tactics left O'Neill jaded. Worse was to come, however,

Fundamentalist Protestant preacher Reverend Ian Paisley (1926–2014) speaking at a rally in 1965. Paisley was a key figure in the Troubles, establishing the Free Presbyterian Church and Democratic Unionist Party. (Photo by Terence Spencer/Popperfoto via Getty Images)

when the UVF murdered several people across Belfast; this inevitably stoked fear and alienation among the Catholic community.

The UVF recruited across working-class Protestant areas. In an interview conducted by the author with one of its founding members, who later became one of its most senior military commanders, he recalled how:

> In the mid-1960s you had the perception that there could be an IRA insurrection and that perception was being fostered by senior Unionist politicians – and people like me 'bit'. With the benefit of hindsight now I wouldn't have.

The UVF was symptomatic of a strain of vigilantism that ran through certain sections of the Protestant community. Although some members of a UVF gang in the Shankill area of West Belfast were arrested and imprisoned for the group's sporadic sectarian attacks in 1966, several other members continued to engage in violence. In 1969 the UVF bombed several targets, including the water supply to Belfast. It was against this background that Terence O'Neill resigned as prime minister in April 1969.

British ambivalence, Irish malevolence

Writing later in his memoir, Terence O'Neill observed how Protestants and Catholics were 'committed by history to live side by side.' He saw it as his mission to 'break the chains of ancient hatreds', though he was unsuccessful at persuading extremists in both communities to accept his agenda for reform. O'Neill's self-belief in reform rather than revolution was fatally undermined by members of his own cabinet hostile to British government interference and by the British government itself. Under the premiership of Harold Wilson, the Labour government (1964–70) frequently claimed that they knew very little about Northern Ireland prior to the explosion of violence in August

1969, although for most of the post-war period the British Labour Party had been kept regularly informed of the situation by their smaller sister party, the Northern Ireland Labour Party (NILP). In his book *A House Divided*, James Callaghan recalled how when he took over as British Home Secretary in 1967 his despatch box

> ...contained books and papers on the future of the prison service, the fire service, problems on race relations, a number of questions about the police, children in care and their future, and the reform of the House of Lords – but not a word about Northern Ireland.

The British government's ignorance of the nature and dynamics of conflict brewing on the streets of Belfast and Derry/Londonderry was matched only by its ambivalence towards the difficulties facing the Stormont government. Unionists understood only too well the precarious

Captain Terence O'Neill (1914–1990), Unionist prime minister in 1963–69, pictured with Labour Prime Minister Harold Wilson. A liberal reformer, O'Neill's modernization agenda was opposed by Paisley, who plotted against him. (Photo by Keystone/Hulton Archive/Getty Images)

NILP leader Tom Boyd pictured with Harold Wilson at Downing Street. The NILP repeatedly warned Wilson of the dangers of political inaction in Ulster but its warnings fell on deaf ears. (Edwards Collection)

foundations upon which their power rested, and they were keen to avoid making concessions. Meanwhile, the Irish government became concerned for the minority community and sought ways to intervene actively on their behalf. Intervention ranged from accommodating northern 'refugees' in camps south of the border, to high-level diplomatic pressure, and the clandestine training and arming of individuals who later went on to form the nucleus of the IRA, carrying out attacks on civilian and military targets.

The stage was now set for confrontation. With open antagonism between unionists and nationalists and with extremists in both communities now seeking to heighten tensions, political inaction in Belfast and London would further drive people to believe their objectives could only be fulfilled by turning to violence.

WARRING SIDES
Brits, Provos and loyalists

The Security Forces

As the sovereign state responsible for security in Northern Ireland, Britain has always sought to portray its role in the conflict as benign, even going to the extent of declaring itself a 'third party' or 'umpire'. Despite protestations to the contrary, however, republicans and nationalists regard Britain as one of the principal parties to the conflict. Far from being a 'neutral arbiter' it was motivated mainly by constitutional interests and by the overwhelming desire to insulate itself from what became, in leading strategic theorist M. L. R. Smith's words, 'the most destabilizing issue in British politics for a generation'. Keeping the Irish conflict 'at arm's length' had been the British government's most consistent policy since the formation of Northern Ireland.

It was unsurprising, then, that the prospect of intervening in the province caused considerable consternation within government circles. James Callaghan hoped that the Unionist administration would not need to invoke the 'military aid to the civil power' provision, though was perceptive enough to commission the Ministry of Defence (MoD) to draw up contingency plans for deploying British troops over the Christmas leave period in 1968–69. On 5 August 1969 the *Belfast Newsletter* reported the presence of troops from the

RUC officers under fire in Derry/ Londonderry on 14 August 1969. Trouble erupted after a Protestant Apprentice Boys' Parade was attacked by nationalists. The police were unprepared for widespread civil disturbances. (Photo by Rolls Press/ Popperfoto via Getty Images/Getty Images)

2nd Battalion of the Queen's Regiment in the RUC station on the Shankill, a rumour that was neither confirmed nor denied by local officials. The troops, reported to be 'specially trained for internal security duties' and with experience in counter-insurgency campaigns in Kenya and Malaya, were returned to the Army's camp, Palace Barracks, after the riots dissipated a few hours later. Terence O'Neill's successor James Chichester-Clark said he 'would be very reluctant to call in British troops at the present time'.

British troops had last been deployed on Northern Ireland's streets during the IRA border campaign on limited operations in support of the RUC. Throughout the six-year offensive their numbers remained constant at 2,500 troops. That figure swelled to 4,000–6,000 upon the outbreak of serious intercommunal violence in mid-August 1969; numbers rose again to 11,243 within a year. Based in Lisburn, the Army's Headquarters Northern Ireland (HQNI) became the operational hub for all military operations in the province. In August

1969, 39 (Infantry) Brigade was established, responsible for Belfast and the eastern part of the province; 8 (Infantry) Brigade took over operational responsibility for the north and west of the province in January 1970, and 3 (Infantry) Brigade oversaw operations in Northern Ireland's southern region.

Northern Ireland presented a wholly novel challenge for British troops. Reflecting on his time as Commanding Officer of the Parachute Regiment's 3rd Battalion (3 Para), in South Armagh during the 1970s, Peter Morton observed how 'soldiering in Northern Ireland is certainly not about aggression, nor fatalism, and indeed many would argue that it is not really soldiering at all'. The British Army tended to rely on tried-and-tested methods of dealing with civil unrest and violence. The troops who were initially deployed to Derry/Londonderry and Belfast advanced to trouble spots in box formation (see page 45), a type of colonial policing technique that afforded troops the opportunity to outmanoeuvre rioters and stop violence before it had a chance to escalate.

British troops were first drawn into major public disorder in October 1969 when members of the Parachute Regiment clashed with local Protestant loyalists in the Shankill Road area of Belfast. (© IWM HU 55869)

British Labour Home Secretary James Callaghan (1912–2005), who had responsibility for authorizing the deployment of troops. Pictured alongside nationalist leader John Hume on 28 August 1969 in the Bogside, Derry/Londonderry. (Part of the Independent Newspapers Ireland/NLI Collection) (Photo by Independent News and Media/Getty Images)

The Army arrived on the streets, therefore, with limited knowledge of the dynamics of the conflict now confronting them, and they depended disproportionately on the experience of members of the RUC who were more familiar with the nuances underpinning the conflict. As one former Royal Engineers soldier who deployed early in Operation *Banner* remarked, 'They were there all the time. It was their home. We were just visitors.' The RUC had 3,000 officers in 1969 and could call on a further 1,500 members of the Ulster Special Constabulary (USC), known as the 'B' Specials, in dire situations. Although the RUC was routinely armed, they had little riot control training and, in the case of the 'B' Specials, there was a general lack of discipline. Following the implementation of the Hunt Report (1969) into policing structures, the Specials were abolished and replaced by the Ulster Defence Regiment (UDR) in 1970, a mostly part-time force that came directly under the British Army's chain of command.

The Provisional IRA

Despite the military failure of its border campaign, the IRA continued to train, arm and equip its members. It intended to bide its time until circumstances changed and the nationalist community was more prepared to support its objectives. Many of those who later joined the IRA after street disturbances in August 1969 would contend that they were propelled into paramilitary ranks because of the circumstances of the time, which made 'ordinary people' do 'extraordinary things'. In an interview with the author, one former IRA member said he joined its ranks when state opposition to civil rights marches cut off the means of peacefully registering protest. 'We tried the force of argument; it didn't work so … it had to be the argument of force.' This was a view shared by a growing number of men and women who recognized that in order to bring about 'a fairer society', things had to be 'deconstructed'. For the former IRA member, 'the only vehicle that could possibly bring that about was the IRA'. While this may

have been the case for many of those younger members who joined the IRA in 1969, there were still those who had joined because they were linked to physical force republicanism through family members who had been involved in one way or another since before the border campaign. The outbreak of the Troubles merely breathed new life into pre-existing structures.

To be sure, the IRA was reborn out of the ashes of Bombay Street, a small, close-knit Catholic community in the shadow of the Roman Catholic Clonard Monastery in West Belfast, which was razed to the ground during severe rioting in August 1969. While its ranks were small, with around 120 members before Bombay Street, by the end of the year the IRA had mushroomed in size to almost 1,000 members. Following a meeting of its ruling Army Council, dissidents in favour of a more proactive defence of beleaguered Catholic communities made their position known, and at a Sinn Féin/IRA Ard Fheis (main meeting) in January 1970 the Republican

Soldiers patrolling in Ardoyne, Belfast, in 1971. Troops were initially welcomed by the Catholic community, though relations soon soured, with the IRA killing its first soldier, Gunner Robert Curtis, on 6 February 1971. (Photo by Terry Fincher/The Fincher Files/Popperfoto via Getty Images)

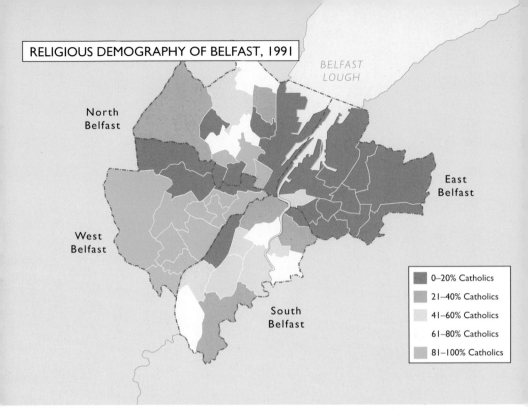

movement formally split. Those who remained behind became known as the Officials and those dissidents who left became known as the Provisionals.

In walking away from existing IRA structures, the Provisionals faced the momentous task of building up a new underground organization. According to evidence he gave at the Saville Inquiry into the shootings perpetrated by the British Army on 30 January 1972 (later known as 'Bloody Sunday'), IRA chief Martin McGuinness estimated that the Provisional IRA in the city of Derry/Londonderry was a small unit, with only 40–50 active members in 1970–71. In an interview with the author, a former leading member of the organization's Belfast Brigade, Tommy Gorman, recalled that although the Provisionals attracted new recruits, for every 300 members in a company, only about five were active:

It was in a pretty bad state. I think in Divis Street that night [1969] there were a couple of short arms and a sub-machine gun. But … at that time it was moribund. And it was in the influx of new recruits and all these older people who had been retired and had gone out back to their farms or something and had suddenly reappeared again and gave us some sort of structure. And it was based on the British Army [structure]. You had companies, battalions and brigades. And companies were based on geographical areas so security was pretty lax. And with the influx of so many new volunteers anybody can sneak in with the rush.

Networks of police, Army and security services informers – or 'touts' as they became known in local parlance – soon penetrated the IRA from top to bottom. Gathering secret information about the IRA and other violent groups was a priority for the security forces from the outset of the Troubles, though the structures and extent of intelligence sharing between the RUC, Army, and Security Service, MI5, was limited. However, as the Provisional IRA grew in size and sophistication, the intelligence picture improved.

Martin McGuinness (left, 1950–2017) was a key architect of the Provisional IRA's terror campaign. From Derry/Londonderry, he later rose to prominence as the group's Chief of Staff and military leader. (Photo by Staff/Mirrorpix/ Getty Images)

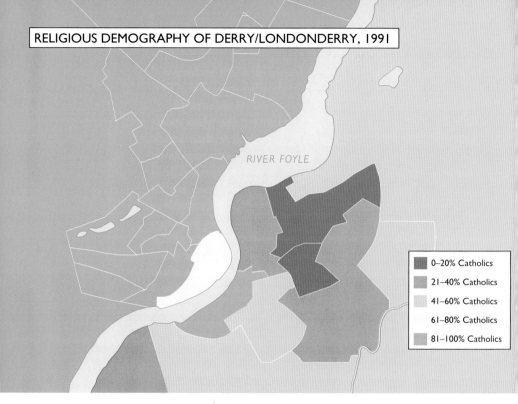

RIVER FOYLE

0–20% Catholics
21–40% Catholics
41–60% Catholics
61–80% Catholics
81–100% Catholics

IRA members came from a variety of backgrounds, though most of the raw recruits, like Gorman, came from working-class areas. Few, if any, had prior military training and the majority joined the IRA following a brush with street violence in their local neighbourhoods. Several were also hardened criminals, who found themselves caught up in republican militancy because of their expertise in procuring funds through illicit means. As J. Bowyer Bell observed in his seminal study on the IRA, *The Secret Army*, '[f]ew Irish rebels are as skilled as the professional soldier – although the protraction of the struggle has meant a rise in standards, standards constantly eroded by losses, lack of training, the needs of the moment, and the failure of corporate memory'. Nonetheless, the IRA was accomplished at portraying its membership as being 'principled soldiers of Ireland'. In its internal Code of Conduct, known to rank-and-file members as the *Green Book*, it warned that '[a]ny Volunteer who brings the Army into disrepute by his/her behaviour may be guilty of a breach of his/her duties and responsibilities as a Volunteer in *Óglaigh na hÉireann* and may be dismissed'.

In terms of weapons and explosives the IRA began as a poorly equipped and ill-disciplined organization. A Provisional IRA member interviewed by the Saville Inquiry recalled how

> ...[t]he weaponry was very ancient to say the least. The Creggan and Bogside units would each have had something like a Thompson [submachine gun], an M1 Carbine, a couple of .303s. There may have been a couple of revolvers as well.

Despite these drawbacks, the IRA would soon emerge as one of the world's most renowned guerrilla armies. Remarkably, much of this transformation would take place within a matter of months.

Loyalist paramilitaries

In contrast to the growing competence and sophistication of the IRA, loyalist paramilitarism was a small-scale affair at the outset of the Troubles. It coalesced mainly around the secretive UVF, re-established in November 1965. By 1971, loyalist paramilitary ranks had ballooned with the formation of the Ulster Defence Association (UDA). The UDA was a huge, unwieldy organization, boasting a membership of over 40,000 by the mid-1970s. Some of its more militant members established an armed wing, the Ulster Freedom Fighters, which killed approximately 259 people between 1971 and 2002. From the outset of the Troubles unionist politicians were worried about vigilantism from within their support base; others, like Stormont Minister for Home Affairs Bill Craig, sought to harness paramilitary muscle for their own political purposes.

By 1974 Protestant militancy had emerged as a formidable force in Northern Ireland politics. The

UVF prisoners pictured in Long Kesh prison in the 1970s. On the right is Billy Mitchell, the group's former Director of Operations, who was captured by the Army in 1976. (Edwards Collection)

UDA provided much of the paramilitary muscle for the Ulster Workers' Council strike in May 1974, which brought down the power-sharing Executive entered into by Brian Faulkner and Gerry Fitt. The Executive was built upon the foundations established by the Sunningdale Agreement in 1973. UDA leaders Andy Tyrie and Glenn Barr believed the Executive gave the Irish government far too much say in Northern Ireland's internal affairs. Along with the UVF, the UDA brought the province to standstill, eventually paving the way for the collapse of power-sharing. The strike effectively 'broke British policy in Ulster', according to veteran journalist Robert Fisk.

In contrast to the UDA's large-scale mobilization for explicitly political purposes, the UVF portrayed itself as a 'counter-terrorist outfit'. Many of its founding members had previous military experience in the British armed forces, with its first commander, Augustus 'Gusty' Spence,

having served in anti-EOKA operations in Cyprus in the late 1950s. One former member had even served in the ranks of the Special Air Service, fighting communist terrorists in Malaya. In the early 1970s several UVF members also belonged to the Territorial Army. It was not long before the UVF began to organize itself along British Army lines. As one former leader revealed in an interview with the author:

> The UVF was formed on a British brigade structure of three battalions, Belfast, Mid Ulster and East Antrim. The idea for the East Antrim Battalion [was that] people believed that it wasn't about the interfaces, it was about the constitution, the future of Northern Ireland, so the UVF was not formed to deal with interfaces, it was formed because they believed there was a sell out, there was a rebellion which had to be stopped. Whether you were from the Shankill or East Antrim you had the one

Augustus 'Gusty' Spence, the former commander of the Shankill Road UVF, pictured after his release from prison in the 1980s. Spence was convicted of shooting dead Peter Ward in 1966. (Pacemaker Press International)

The UVF was formed in 1965, predating the Provisional IRA's emergence in 1970. The group portrayed itself as a 'counter-terrorist outfit', though in reality it also indiscriminately targeted Catholic civilians. (Edwards Collection)

enemy – the IRA. Indeed, the nationalist community [more broadly were considered the enemy], as most UVF volunteers didn't distinguish between the IRA and those they fought for.

Over the course of the Troubles the UVF would be directly responsible for almost 500 deaths; 84 per cent of its victims were civilians, 10 per cent were other loyalists, 5 per cent were republicans and 1 per cent were Security Forces personnel. Loyalist paramilitaries were eventually to prove themselves as ruthless as their republican opponents in prosecuting their armed campaigns.

OUTBREAK
Politics in the streets

Formed in 1967, the Northern Ireland Civil Rights Association (NICRA) sought a redistribution of employment, housing, and voting rights for all. Mostly made up of Catholic nationalists, republicans, agnostic socialists and liberals, NICRA initially had a handful of Protestants in its ranks; however, following a violent clash between marchers and police in Derry/Londonderry's Duke Street on 5 October 1968 most Protestants left. Many civil rights marches were already illegal, but the withdrawal of law-abiding Protestant citizens – whose presence gave the movement a degree of political protection – did not deter it from using dangerously confrontational tactics to draw attention to its cause. Nor did it deter its leaders from demanding concessions – such as the abolition of the Special Powers Act and the disbandment of the 'B' Specials – from the Stormont administration.

In the view of UVF leaders like Billy Mitchell, interviewed by the author, NICRA was really only seeking 'civil rights for Catholics'. Mitchell, a committed follower of the Reverend Ian Paisley in the 1960s and 1970s, had joined the UVF in 1970, rising through its ranks to become the group's Director of Military Operations a few years later. He described how unionist politicians repeatedly warned loyalists that an IRA threat existed in the 1960s; republicans, they were told, had infiltrated the ranks of the civil rights movement. Evidence for such claims was readily available. The IRA's Chief of Staff, Sean Garland, had been arrested in Dublin in 1966, along with a document that outlined how the IRA intended to subvert trades unions and other bodies established to lobby for socio-economic reform, and prompt them to push for a united Ireland. It was just what Paisley had been warning about. Suddenly the latent risk posed by the IRA after its border campaign fizzled out became a real threat in the minds of many unionists. NICRA became tainted by association.

What made matters worse was that the tribalism associated with marching was deeply ingrained in the psyche of both communities. By insisting on walking through majority Protestant areas, NICRA's leaders actually fanned the flames of resentment between the two communities. Many Protestants observing the civil rights movement could not understand why Catholics were seeking a radical redistribution of rights that most working-class people – of whatever creed – did not themselves enjoy. Furthermore, Protestants saw the attacks on the RUC and the 'B' Specials as a direct attack on *their* state.

Violence increased markedly during the hot summer of 1969 as Orange Order marches got under way. Of the nine people who lost their lives in July and August, six were killed by the RUC, one by the 'B' Specials, one by loyalists and another by republicans. The atmosphere became electric. The use of machine guns by the RUC – particularly in enclosed urban areas – bordered on recklessness and alarmed many people, including politicians in London. Nine-year-old Patrick Rooney was shot and killed in his bed by a .30-calibre bullet, fired from a Browning M1919A4 machine gun mounted on top of an RUC Shorland armoured car. One eyewitness later interviewed by the author said that the use of such weaponry by the police led many local people to believe that 'an even greater loss of life had been incurred' than was actually the case. Although the death toll was surprisingly low given the sheer intensity of the street violence, perception was everything, and it fed a vicious cycle. Sectarian confrontation fanned the flames of violence as politics once again returned to the streets of Northern Ireland.

The British Army arrives

At approximately 1635 hours on the afternoon of 14 August 1969, a request was made by the RUC's Inspector General for the immediate deployment of troops to support the civil power in Northern Ireland. Home Secretary James Callaghan received the message from Whitehall mid-flight as he made his way back to Wiltshire from a meeting with Prime Minister Harold Wilson. Radioing back to London, he quickly granted permission for the use of troops.

The first unit deployed to Derry/Londonderry was 1st Battalion, The Prince of Wales's Own Regiment of Yorkshire, with orders to relieve exhausted members of

British Army platoon box formation

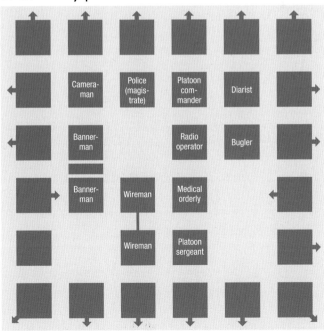

The Army's box formation tactic, used in riot control situations, proved short-lived in Northern Ireland as the violence grew towards the troops in ferocity.

British troops deployed onto the streets of Belfast on 15 August 1969, initially to keep the peace between warring factions. They would remain there for 38 years. (Photo by Popperfoto via Getty Images/Getty Images)

the RUC and 'B' Specials and to keep the peace between two warring communities. A statement issued by the British government at the time read:

> The GOC [General Officer Commanding] N. Ireland has been instructed to take all necessary steps, acting

impartially between citizen and citizen, to restore law
and order. Troops will be withdrawn as soon as this is
accomplished. This is a limited operation and during it
troops will remain under the direct and exclusive control
of the GOC who will continue to be responsible to the
UK Government.

No sooner had violence been brought under control in Derry/Londonderry than it flared up in Belfast. On the night of 14/15 August the sound of gunfire and exploding bombs in the province's two main cities could be heard amid an upsurge in intercommunal rioting between Protestants and Catholics. Following a desperate appeal by West Belfast nationalist MP Gerry Fitt for further troop deployment, the Home Secretary remarked, 'Gerry, I can get the Army in but it's going to be a devil of a job to get it out.'

As Fitt's appeal suggested, Catholics were open to the deployment of soldiers when they first arrived in August 1969. Those soldiers who found themselves marching into the Falls Road area were met with cheers and cups of tea and plates of sandwiches. There was a belief that the troops had come to save the beleaguered community from being attacked by Protestant extremists and members of the RUC and 'B' Specials. A few weeks later the GOC Northern Ireland, Lieutenant-General Sir Ian Freeland, told a press conference that if a political solution uniting Belfast and London could not be found, then 'the honeymoon period could finish in a matter of hours. Our soldiers, in between the rival factions in Belfast, might become the target of both sides.' Freeland's observations proved accurate. The relationship soon soured, first in Derry/Londonderry and then in Belfast, as the Army was accused of standing aside while loyalist militants ransacked and burned Catholic homes. Following a meeting between influential members of the Catholic community, which included Fitt and Stormont NILP MP for the Falls Road Paddy Devlin, Callaghan issued a press release in which he made it clear that 'General Freeland had assured him that by means of the peace line and in other ways the Army would afford all reasonable protection for whatever period it was necessary'. Indeed, the Army attempted to reach an agreement at a local level with both communities about dismantling barricades. Nevertheless, the intensity of the intercommunal violence made establishing a 'peace line' – makeshift barbed-wire fences, later to become

permanent walls – the only way to keep both sides apart, especially in Belfast where Protestants and Catholics lived in close proximity.

The Army had deployed to the province with little knowledge of the nature of the conflict between Protestants and Catholics. To address this deficit they applied tried-and-tested techniques from colonial theatres in an attempt to quell the violence. The columns of soldiers marching up Shipquay Street in Derry City in box formation illustrated this well; so too did the apocryphal tale of a banner being unfurled on the streets with instructions in Arabic to 'disperse or we fire' emblazoned on it. Public-order training was an integral component of the Army's Internal Security doctrine (compilation of best practice) at the time. For individual soldiers, only the most senior NCOs and

Lieutenant-General Sir Ian Freeland was the Army's top military commander in Northern Ireland, 1969–71. Pictured here greeting troops disembarking at a naval base in Derry/Londonderry in September 1969. (Photo by Mirrorpix/Mirrorpix via Getty Images)

officers would have had combat experience in the last major deployment, Aden, two years earlier.

Two weeks after he authorized the deployment of troops, James Callaghan arrived in Belfast for talks with Northern Ireland's prime minister, James Chichester-Clark, on the package of reforms negotiated between the two governments in London and Belfast. Callaghan visited the areas worst hit by rioting, reassuring Catholics on a visit to the Bogside in Derry/Londonderry that he would 'bend all his endeavours' towards ensuring that all citizens of Northern Ireland would enjoy justice and equality and freedom from fear. When he returned again a few weeks later he announced the findings of the Hunt Report, which recommended the disbandment of the 'B' Specials and the disarmament of the RUC. It was too little, too late. Catholics were soon calling for more than reform of the state, with some even beginning to look to the IRA to provide a physical force solution to the problem.

The violence escalates

The short-lived Northern Ireland Community Relations Commission estimated that in 1971 alone 2,069 families moved out of their homes across Belfast because of political violence. The areas worst affected included the predominantly Catholic districts of Ardoyne and Clonard, where 363 families left, and the Grosvenor Road and Roden Street area, where 225 families sought refuge elsewhere. Most families who moved out of these areas were Protestant, while in Ballysillan the overwhelming outflow was made up of Catholic families. The South Belfast area of Suffolk was worst hit: over 88 per cent of those who moved out were Protestant. The Commission's report concluded that the biggest population shift in Western Europe since 1945 was caused by an 'overpowering sense of insecurity and fear'. However, these figures were dwarfed by the population movement in Derry/Londonderry. In 1971 there were 8,459 Protestants living in the west side of the city; by

1981 that figure had dropped to 2,874, and by 1991 it had plummeted again to 1,407. This represented a staggering population decline of 83.4 per cent.

Some unionists thought that the Stormont government had lost control of the situation and was allowing the province to slip into chaos and anarchy. In a letter to Chichester-Clark on 27 September 1969 Dr Norman Laird, the Stormont MP for Belfast St Anne's, summed up the feelings of his supporters when he warned:

> I am quite satisfied the Cabinet does not know the extent of the very bitter resentment throughout the Country. Loyalists have been extremely patient and tolerant but the limit of toleration is not far off, and if the loyalists really rise up in anger the resulting explosion all over the Country will make what has happened so far look like a child's picnic.

Such apocalyptic language was commonplace among the unionist grassroots. Something had to be done, and quickly. A new front now opened up as Protestant extremists began to establish their own vigilante organizations.

A mural in Canada Street, Belfast, depicting Protestants being driven from their homes by Catholics. Violence on both sides drove purportedly the biggest population shift in Western Europe since 1945. (Edwards Collection)

THE FIGHTING
From counter-insurgency to internal security

The tempo of armed conflict in Northern Ireland fluctuated according to the broader political picture. Violence spiked at times of great intercommunal strife and dipped at times when political breakthroughs seemed within reach. Throughout the long years of Operation *Banner* the Army was issued with a number of political directives from Whitehall, which firmly subordinated military operations to the government's wider policy goals. For most of the Troubles the government's objective was to provide security to the people of Northern Ireland while seeking a long-term political solution to the dispute between Protestants and Catholics over the future of the province.

On the military front, Operation *Banner* ebbed and flowed as the threat from terrorism itself evolved. In 1969 and 1970 the Army kept a tentative peace, while the decision by the IRA to go on the offensive by killing soldiers and police officers in 1971 saw British troops respond with a counter-insurgency drive. With the advent of 'police primacy' in 1977, the Army's role would be scaled back over the remaining 30 years of Operation *Banner* to one of providing military support to the RUC in counter-terrorist operations.

Countering insurgency

The escalation of violence that gripped Northern Ireland in 1971 posed a number of difficulties for military commanders on the ground. One of General Freeland's successors, Lieutenant-General Sir Harry Tuzo, who served as GOC between 1971 and 1973, was a seasoned soldier more accustomed to operating in colonial theatres like Borneo than the domestic surroundings of Northern Ireland. Like the soldiers he commanded, Tuzo's operational experience taught him who the enemy was, why they were the enemy, and above all how to apply the right amount of military force in order to defeat them. In Belfast and Derry/Londonderry, the centre of gravity in the relationship between the troops and the people began to shift and it was proving infinitely more difficult to win over the 'hearts and minds' of the local Catholic population. What made matters worse was that the Army effectively worked to two masters – one in London and one in Belfast – allowing the IRA to portray the troops less as peacekeepers and more as ardent enforcers of the will of the local Unionist regime. The IRA, backed up by the newly swollen ranks of disaffected nationalist youths, embarked on a campaign of armed propaganda to counter the Army's claims to be seeking to win their hearts and minds.

In coming face-to-face with the civil disobedience engulfing the province, General Tuzo was determined to tackle the threat head on. He dismissed criticism from influential unionists in border areas that his troops were not doing enough to protect them or that the Security Forces had all but adopted a defensive posture. 'Anti-guerrilla tactics,' he wrote to one government representative at the time, 'often appear in this light, especially in a civilised community where the rule of common law still has a part to play'. Tuzo concluded perceptively, '[t]he hard fact is that in guerrilla war the enemy holds the initiative for large parts of the time and information is the key to his defeat'. Without the support of key sections of the population the flow of information soon dried up and the Army found itself fighting blind.

British troops impose a curfew on the Falls Road, a predominantly Catholic area of Belfast, on 3–5 July 1970. The operation was designed to remove illegal weapons from terrorist hands. (Photo by Malcolm Stroud/Express/Getty Images)

In the Bogside in Derry/Londonderry, as in so many ghettoized areas across the province, the Catholic population had now turned against Tuzo's soldiers. The 'honeymoon period' enjoyed by the troops following their initial deployment in 1969 ended abruptly and without any real prospect of reconciliation. Instead of being treated to cups of tea and sandwiches by Catholic housewives, British soldiers were now greeted with gunfire, bombs and widespread civil disorder.

Early attempts to quell rioting – or 'aggro' as soldiers called it – were clumsy. Large-scale cordon-and-search operations served only to alienate Catholic working-class opinion. Furthermore, the Army's ability to respond to the embryonic IRA propaganda campaign was amateurish, and, in the words of one former Army staff officer based on the press desk in HQNI, speaking to the author, it 'simply had not been thought through'. In all this General Tuzo was working at a disadvantage. The Stormont and London governments were constantly quarrelling over security matters. The confusing political signals made it much more difficult for the soldiers operating on the ground whose advice Stormont ministers were reluctant to accept. This was to have tragic repercussions in the early 1970s.

In a cordon-and-search operation known popularly ever since as 'the Falls Road curfew', Tuzo's predecessor General Ian Freeland reluctantly ordered soldiers into the Lower Falls in Belfast on 3 July 1970 to search for IRA weapons. In the unfolding drama, rioting broke out, the air became thick with plumes of smoke billowing from burning vehicles and homes, and soldiers fired numerous CS gas canisters to disperse the crowd. The CS gas drifted into residential homes, choking their occupants, many of whom were desperately trying to carve out an ordinary existence for themselves amid the chaos. Matters were made infinitely worse when a curfew was imposed, which confined people to their homes, playing straight into the IRA's hands.

As a result of these earlier, coercive operations, Tuzo and his deputy, Major-General Robert Ford, soon found themselves confronted with the perennial difficulty of drawing out the insurgents into a clash with the Security Forces, especially since they were now firmly embedded in a community who had begun to see the IRA as their defenders. However, this was by no means the same story across Northern Ireland. The majority Protestant population wished to maintain the Union between Northern Ireland and Great Britain and they generally supported the Security Forces. Yet for a sizeable minority, concentrated in areas increasingly hostile to the Unionist regime, the fight was less clear-cut. The conundrum facing Tuzo and Ford in Northern Ireland was to take over a quarter of a century to solve.

Although the British Army's own thinking on counter-insurgency at this time was extensive, it had been a direct product of the Army's involvement in

Troops carry out a controlled explosion on a suspect vehicle in Belfast on 17 November 1971. Car bombs were used frequently by terrorists on both sides during the Troubles. (Photo by Keystone/Getty Images)

colonial territories like Palestine, Malaya, Kenya, Cyprus and Aden. While it was extensive, it would be wrong to think of it as highly successful. In some of these places, like Aden between 1963 and 1967, the Army had been slow to respond to the armed campaign fought by the National Liberation Front. As it would come to realize in Northern Ireland, without a sophisticated understanding of the conflict dynamics, force would always be limited

in terms of what it could provide by way of a solution to
a deterioration of the security situation.

In the early 1970s the Army's doctrine characterized
all insurgents, regardless of where they could be found
in the world, in the following terms:

> The insurgent is usually careless of death. He has no mental
> doubts, is little troubled by humanitarian sentiments, and

is not moved by slaughter and mutilation. His upbringing
and standard of living make him well fitted to hardship.
He requires little sustenance and comfort, and can look
after himself. The insurgent has a keen and practised eye
for country and has the ability to move across it, at speed,
on his feet. He is capable of being trained to use modern
and complicated weapons to good effect.

The Army may have been well equipped to fight an
arduous guerrilla war in these colonial contexts, but
in the heart of British cities such as Belfast and Derry/
Londonderry it was a different matter. The Army's
carelessness, mixed with the republican penchant for
drawing historic parallels from several hundred years of
perceived injustice, contributed to an explosive situation.

Republican actions soon became more aggressive.
In contrast to the largely defensive posture adopted in
1969–70, the Provisional IRA Army Council issued an
order in January 1971 to conduct offensive operations
against the Security Forces. The first soldier to lose his
life was Gunner Robert Curtis, who was ambushed by
an IRA unit commanded by Billy Reid from the New
Lodge Road on 6 February 1971. Gunner Curtis's troop
was on public order duty, trying to prevent a mob from
attacking people at the New Lodge/Tiger's Bay interface.
The crowd broke up to allow an IRA gunman to throw
a nail bomb, which was closely followed by a long burst
of automatic fire. The crowd then re-formed to prevent
soldiers from giving chase. Four of Gunner Curtis's
comrades were also injured. Reid was later killed when
he attempted to ambush another British Army patrol on
15 May 1971, ironically at the corner of Curtis Street/
Academy Street, behind St Anne's Cathedral.

The IRA also shifted its operations from direct
confrontations with the military on the streets to targeted
assassinations of off-duty soldiers. The brutal murders of
three young Scottish soldiers (two of them brothers) aged
17, 18 and 23 on 10 March 1971 at Ligoniel, North
Belfast, graphically illustrated the extent to which the
IRA was determined to 'blood' its volunteers. Lured to

their deaths by two female IRA members after a night out, each of the young men was shot in the back of the head by gunmen as they relieved themselves by the side of a quiet country road. It was not to be the last time that the 'honey-trap' tactic was used by republicans. On 23 March 1973 female terrorists again lured four off-duty soldiers to a house on the Antrim Road, with the pretext of attending a party. No sooner had the women left the house than IRA gunmen burst in and frogmarched the soldiers to one of the bedrooms, where they were all told to kneel down facing the bed. The gunmen then opened fire with an automatic rifle. Two soldiers were killed instantly and the third died of his wounds a short time later; the fourth soldier miraculously survived. The IRA repeated the 'honey-trap' ploy again in 1981, when one soldier was murdered and another seriously wounded in similar circumstances. Such ruthless killings had echoes of the tactics used by Jewish insurgents against British forces in Palestine in the 1940s.

By Easter 1971, the Army was dealing with mass rioting, endless blast and nail bombings, the erection of barricades and countless gun battles with IRA and loyalist gunmen on a daily basis. In its first deployment in the Lower Falls area the 3rd Battalion of the Royal Anglian Regiment found itself amidst an escalating cycle of violence. Its Tactical Area of Responsibility bordered the Protestant Shankill to the north, the Grosvenor in the south, the Upper Falls/Springfield Road to the west, and Millfield to the east. As a flavour of what units on emergency tours could expect, on 19 April 1971 alone, 177 shots were fired at the battalion. In its four months in Northern Ireland, the Royal Anglians suffered four fatalities and 36 wounded.

Army units tended to counter such violence on an ad hoc basis, their tactics dictated by operational circumstances. However, from time to time in the early 1970s the Army was ordered by politicians in London to mount major operations. Perhaps the most counter-productive of these was internment (known by its military codename Operation *Demetrius*), which saw province-wide sweeps designed to capture senior members of the IRA. In an interview with the author, one former Army officer present at a briefing of all commanders operating within 39 (Infantry) Brigade – which had responsibility for Belfast – on the morning of 9 August 1971 recalled overhearing a more senior officer tell his subordinates in a confident mood that 'today is the beginning of the end for the IRA' and that 'without the head, the body will simply thrash around and eventually die'. The same officer talked to a sergeant from the Parachute Regiment at Palace Barracks shortly after the initial round-ups, who made the contrasting observation that 'for every one we picked up we have recruited ten for the IRA'. Initially doubtful of the strategic benefits of internment, the Army nonetheless set about implementing the political will of the London government – pressured by new Northern Ireland premier Brian Faulkner – in arresting and detaining suspects.

However, there were signs that within six months, HQNI was warming to the idea of relaxing the security measure in order to curry favour with the Catholic minority, as one secret letter to No. 10 Downing Street made clear:

> The Army recognise that the political initiative which is taken with the object of recapturing the confidence of the Catholic community, while retaining that of the Protestants, will have to include some move on internment if the initiative is to stand any chance of succeeding – and it is of course very much in the Army's interest that it should succeed.

Historians have since uncovered evidence to suggest that the Army was politically sensitive to the non-military remedies proposed to end the violence. Nevertheless, there remains a question mark over the extent to which it could hope to influence government policy. The Army, like other elements of the Security Forces, was the servant of its political masters. In any case, due to outdated intelligence, some key IRA leaders slipped the net and

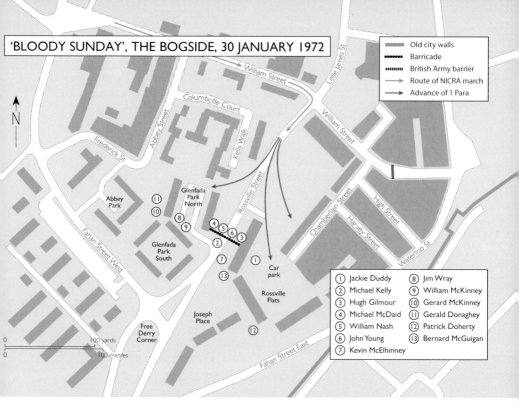

'BLOODY SUNDAY', THE BOGSIDE, 30 JANUARY 1972

Old city walls
Barricade
British Army barrier
Route of NICRA march
Advance of 1 Para

① Jackie Duddy   ⑧ Jim Wray
② Michael Kelly   ⑨ William McKinney
③ Hugh Gilmour   ⑩ Gerard McKinney
④ Michael McDaid   ⑪ Gerald Donaghey
⑤ William Nash   ⑫ Patrick Doherty
⑥ John Young   ⑬ Bernard McGuigan
⑦ Kevin McElhinney

internment had only limited effects in preventing the IRA from establishing itself in Catholic areas.

Other factors that shaped the Army's decision-making on internment including the allegations of inhumane and degrading treatment of terrorist suspects and other detainees arrested by the Security Forces. Loose guidelines on tactical questioning led to harsh treatment and the use of what were known as the 'Five Techniques' – i.e. hooding detainees, placing them in stress positions, and subjecting them to white noise, sleep deprivation and a limited diet of bread and water – which led to a public outcry. An inquiry led by Sir Edmund Compton was established to investigate these allegations. Compton found that while there had been physical ill-treatment, such as the application of the five techniques, there was insufficient evidence of brutality. Against a backdrop of such negative publicity, the Army was fast becoming an agent of oppression in the eyes of the nationalist community.

One of the Army's most controversial operations was that undertaken by the 1st Battalion of the Parachute Regiment (1 Para), on 30 January 1972. Later known as 'Bloody Sunday', it was an arrest operation launched to round up suspected ringleaders of the violence that frequently accompanied illegal civil rights marches. Within 30 minutes of 1 Para entering the nationalist Bogside, 27 people had been shot, 13 fatally, with one person dying of wounds two weeks later. The episode poisoned relations between the Army and the nationalist community, providing a 'recruiting sergeant' for the IRA. The very use of the label 'Bloody Sunday' conjured up parallels with the Black and Tans' shooting of 12 Irish civilians in Croke Park, Dublin, on Sunday 21 November 1920.

Gun and bomb attacks increased in frequency across Northern Ireland after Bloody Sunday. In 1972 alone 497 people would be killed as a result of the Troubles and 4,876 injured. Fourteen per cent of these deaths were concentrated in North Belfast, with the remainder

Youths confront soldiers minutes before members of the 1st Battalion of the Parachute Regiment open fire on protestors on 'Bloody Sunday', 30 January 1972, in Derry/Londonderry. Fourteen civilians were killed. (Photo by William L. Rukeyser/Getty Images)

spread evenly across Belfast, Derry/Londonderry City and South Armagh. In the two years after Bloody Sunday there would be approximately 15,650 shootings and 2,360 bomb explosions.

The Provisional IRA bombing campaign

Bombs were the IRA's main weapon of choice. There were countless incidents throughout the 38 years of Operation *Banner* involving the use of explosives (from the IRA's coordinated attacks on Security Forces patrols by way of fertilizer bombs and Semtex shaped charges), Improvised Explosive Devices (IEDs), mortars, blast bombs, under-car booby-trap bombs and mines. In the early 1970s the IRA's explosives were typically constructed using what some IRA members called 'over-the-counter' methods. As one former bomb-maker revealed in an interview with the author:

> In the initial parts of the struggle all of our explosives were homemade. We called it co-op mix because you could have got it in the corner shop. There were different mixes. Benzene mixes, diesel mix with fertilizer and stuff like that …

The devastating impact that these commercial-based explosive devices were to have on ordinary people was unparalleled in contemporary Northern Irish history. The IRA was pioneering a deadly ingenuity of a kind that could target individuals with booby-trap bombs at home and at work, to car bombs that were so powerful they could destroy buildings. For the IRA, bombs offered an effective tool for killing people as well as, crucially, spreading fear and damaging Northern Ireland's economy. One of the early proponents of these weapons was Martin McGuinness, who personally led a bombing campaign against commercial targets in Derry/Londonderry.

In response to the IRA's bombing campaign the Army formed 321 Explosive Ordnance Disposal (EOD) Company, which drew its operators from the ranks of

A remote-controlled wheelbarrow robot of 321 EOD Company, Royal Logistics Corps, carries out a controlled explosion on a suspect car bomb. Several EOD operators died in the line of duty. (© IWM HU 47328)

the Royal Army Ordnance Corps. Between 1969 and 1992, 321 EOD Company dealt with over 40,000 emergency calls, averaging about 40 per week. In 1991 the organization defused an 8,000lb (3,629kg) proxy bomb, the biggest bomb ever made safe in Northern Ireland, near the Annaghmartin Permanent Vehicle Checkpoint (PVCP). The first Army Technical Officer (ATO) to be killed was 29-year-old Captain David Stewartson, who was blown up attempting to defuse a bomb on 9 September 1971. In 1972 six EOD operators were killed in explosions, representing 50 per cent of the unit's operators killed during the Troubles. The IRA's reputation as a terrorist organization capable of inflicting huge damage by explosive devices was not built overnight. In the early 1970s the IRA scored numerous 'own goals', whereby inexperienced and poorly trained bomb-makers blew themselves up while constructing, transporting and planting bombs. For instance, in February 1972 two republicans, Patrick Casey and Eamonn Gamble, blew themselves up while tinkering

with a bomb at temporary council offices in a school hall in Keady. Two other IRA members, aged 19 and 20, were killed when the bomb they were transporting exploded prematurely, leaving their vehicle in a tangled mess in King Street, Magherafelt. In Crumlin, near Lough Neagh, two IRA volunteers died when the bomb they were transporting by barge exploded, killing both of them instantly. Four more IRA members died when the bomb they were transporting along the Knockbreda Road went off, obliterating their car.

On 9 March 1972 four members of the IRA's 2nd Belfast Battalion working with explosives in a house on the Falls Road died when they crossed the wrong wire on a detonator switch. On 7 April three other IRA men (all aged 17) died when they blew themselves up in Bawnmore Park in North Belfast. A devastating premature explosion on 28 May claimed the lives of a further four IRA volunteers and four civilians, underlining the dangers of working in enclosed residential surroundings. Three more IRA men met a similar fate at the beginning of August, as did three of their comrades and six innocent civilians, when a premature explosion ripped through the customs office at Newry. Thirteen more IRA men and six others were to die in similar incidents before the end of the year. These 'own goals' highlighted the inherent danger of using the bomb as a lethal weapon in close proximity to the civilian population.

Although the deaths of IRA bomb makers by their own hand removed key people from the IRA's ranks, it did not prevent other bombers from hitting their targets. Six Protestants and one Catholic died when the IRA exploded a car bomb in Donegall Street, Belfast, on 20 March 1972. An inadequate warning had been given by the IRA. It was fairly representative of the IRA's campaign at the time.

With an upsurge in violent attacks in the first half of 1972, the British government attempted to find alternative ways to deal with the IRA. In early July 1972 an IRA delegation, including Ballymurphy republican Gerry Adams, who was on remand in Long Kesh prison

The panic-stricken faces of those running for their lives as the IRA detonates no-warning car bombs in Belfast on 21 July 1972. Nine people were killed in the bomb blitz. (Photo by Daily Mirror/Mirrorpix/Mirrorpix via Getty Images)

camp, and Derry IRA commander Martin McGuinness, were flown to London for a secret meeting with William Whitelaw, the Secretary of State for Northern Ireland. The talks amounted to little and the truce declared by the IRA was terminated against the backdrop of a renewed armed offensive.

On 21 July 1972 the IRA exploded 22 no-warning car bombs across Belfast in a blitz that saw six soldiers, two civilians and a UDA member die and over 130 people injured within an area with a one-mile radius. The bomb blitz provoked massive outrage, particularly because it now appeared that the IRA was deliberately targeting civilians.

Against the increasingly indiscriminate nature of paramilitary violence, the Ministry of Defence issued a more comprehensive set of Rules of Engagement (ROE) for soldiers in Northern Ireland. Known more commonly as the 'yellow card', these new ROE gave troops the option to return fire if their lives were threatened (i.e. for self-defence purposes) and as long as, in their own judgement, they believed there to be a threat. As the ROE explained: 'Soldiers may fire without warning if there is no other way to protect themselves or those whom it is their duty to protect from the danger of being killed or seriously injured.' Owing to the high intensity of gun and bomb attacks, the ROE also authorized troops to use heavy weapons under certain circumstances:

> … a company commander may order the firing of heavy weapons (such as the Carl Gustav [a recoilless rifle]) against positions from which there is sustained hostile firing, if he believes that this is necessary for the preservation of the lives of soldiers or of other persons whom it is his duty to protect. In deciding whether or not to use heavy weapons full account must be taken of the risk that the opening of fire may endanger the lives of innocent persons.

The Yellow Card had originally been issued to soldiers in September 1969 and was revised again three times by

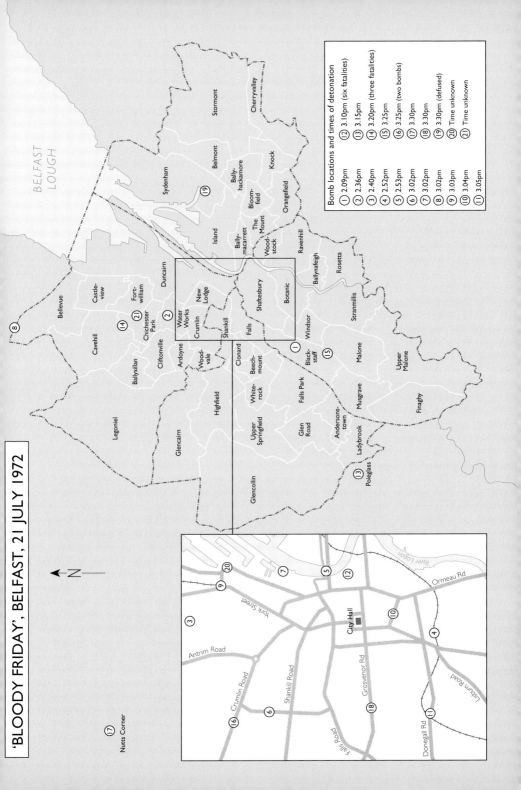

'BLOODY FRIDAY', BELFAST, 21 JULY 1972

Bomb locations and times of detonation

① 2.09pm
② 2.36pm
③ 2.40pm (three fatalities)
④ 2.52pm
⑤ 2.53pm
⑥ 3.25pm (two bombs)
⑦ 3.02pm
⑧ 3.02pm
⑨ 3.03pm
⑩ 3.04pm
⑪ 3.05pm
⑫ 3.10pm (six fatalities)
⑬ 3.15pm
⑭ 3.20pm (three fatalities)
⑮ 3.25pm
⑯ 3.25pm (two bombs)
⑰ 3.30pm
⑱ 3.30pm
⑲ 3.30pm (defused)
⑳ Time unknown
㉑ Time unknown

November 1971. It would be tightened up again in July 1972, a few months after the Bloody Sunday shootings.

That soldiers were permitted to open fire with aimed shots only when someone was deliberately shooting at them and even then with a minimum use of force led to claims that the Army was operating with one hand tied behind its back. When considered in the context of an escalation of IRA violence, it left the British government with a dilemma. On the one hand public opinion at home was largely supportive of the troops, while nationalist opinion and those who had sympathy with them elsewhere meant the government had to walk a fine line. As a Top Secret minute of the British Cabinet indicated:

> The anger of the Protestant community had been such that, if he [the prime minister] and the Secretary of State for Defence had not immediately authorised sterner measures by the security forces against the IRA, there would have been a very serious risk of direct action on the streets on a widespread scale. The operations that had been undertaken had done much to calm Protestant opinion; nevertheless they had made no more than modest inroads upon the operational capability of the IRA, and had predictably caused some alienation of Roman Catholic opinion.

It was decided in London that the Army should mount a major operation codenamed *Motorman* that was designed to retake so-called 'no-go areas' in Belfast and Derry/Londonderry.

In Derry/Londonderry the local 8 (Infantry) Brigade had nine regular infantry battalions, two UDR battalions, two Royal Engineer field squadrons, a troop of four Centurion AVREs (Armoured Vehicles Royal Engineers, a version of the Centurion tank) and a further seven minor units at its disposal for the operation. Under cover of darkness the units moved into position on 31 July 1972. The operation was given the green light at 0400 hours. The infantry battalions, closely supported

by the Combat Engineers, moved quickly to dominate their Tactical Areas of Responsibility and remove the barricades. In a radio broadcast, William Whitelaw made clear the government's intention to restore law and order by any means necessary, thus ensuring that the IRA was given adequate warning of the impending military incursions. As with many earlier head-on engagements, the IRA chose to retreat to its safe havens across the border. Only token resistance was met by the Army as Operation *Motorman* swung into action. One civilian and one unarmed IRA member were killed. By now troops were saturating Belfast and Derry/Londonderry, taking all their objectives by 0730 hours.

As a way of distracting troops from their main objective of clearing 'no-go areas' in Derry/Londonderry, the IRA exploded three no-warning car bombs in the

A British Centurion tank smashes down a barricade in the Creggan Estate, Derry/Londonderry during Operation *Motorman* on 31 July 1972. *Motorman* was aimed at dismantling so-called 'No Go areas'. (Photo by Popperfoto via Getty Images/Getty Images)

small village of Claudy, not far from the city. Nine people were killed, including a child.

Although Operation *Motorman* inflicted a short-term defeat on the IRA in both cities, it did not make the organization any less dangerous in other parts of Northern Ireland. In an incident at Sanaghanroe near Dungannon at 2300 hours on 10 September 1972, three soldiers from 1st Battalion, The Argyll and Sutherland Highlanders, were killed and four injured when their Saracen armoured personnel carrier was blown up. All those killed were in their early twenties. The sheer force of the blast lifted the armoured vehicle off the ground and threw it 15–20 yards through a hedge and into a field. The bomb attack left a crater 30ft in diameter and 12–15ft deep. In this incident the IRA's firing point was 70–80 yards away, up a hill within sight of the road. Two weeks later another bomb was detonated directly in front of a Saracen armoured vehicle, causing the same devastating result; remarkably, the two soldiers escaped with only minor injuries. In total the IRA carried out 1,200 operations in 1972, mainly in rural areas of the province.

Republicans carried out over 35 IED attacks on the Army in August 1972 alone. As one confidential Army report from the time put it, 'The tactics of the IRA may change as a result of Op MOTORMAN and attacks on the Security Forces in the rural areas could increase; the increased use of command detonated mines is all too likely'. The command-detonated IED was the commonest weapon in the IRA's armoury and would become more sophisticated as the conflict progressed. Such bombs were typically constructed using 200–300lb (91–136kg) of explosive packed into a milk churn and placed under a culvert or dug into a grass verge at the side of a road. They were detonated by command wire and (later) remote-firing mechanisms, causing massive carnage. These devices had far-reaching effects on the military's movement on the ground. In an interview with the author one soldier who survived an IRA attack described how it felt:

One night on patrol in County Londonderry we were travelling along in our vehicles and we heard a bang. We immediately assumed that it was a contact. Our Royal Engineers Search Adviser later came out and, after surveying the scene, informed us that it had been a 1,000lb [454kg] bomb, which had detonated as we passed over a culvert, narrowly missing us. We had a few lucky escapes.

In response to the growing number of military casualties caused by roadside bombs, the MoD gave more careful consideration to the use of helicopters to ferry troops around on operations. In one threat assessment the Army concluded that the main tactical weapon in the IRA's armoury was its volunteers' ability to withdraw hastily after carrying out armed actions by exploiting their knowledge of the local terrain:

An Army unit confronted by rioters in Derry/ Londonderry. The military developed the tactical use of baton guns, instead of live ammunition, to meet the political sensitives of the local situation. (Alain Le Garsmeur "The Troubles" Archive / Alamy Stock Photo)

Terrorist tactics are normally based on hit-and-run techniques both on foot and in cars. Ambushes, whether from which to snipe or command-detonate a mine, are relatively easy to set up but depend for their success on the availability of a rapid method of withdrawal. Withdrawal routes are often over fields where the terrorist has too great a head start on Security Force pursuers, or along nearby roads which cannot be reached quickly enough by Security Force vehicles which are, in any case, unsuited to chase getaway cars.

Use of helicopters increased and was soon exploited for other ends too, particularly since the Gazelle model provided a continuously available airborne reconnaissance and surveillance platform.

There were practical advantages to using the helicopter as a troop transporter, which 2 Para's experience in South Armagh on its third emergency tour bears out. Deployed on 27 March 1973 to what Merlyn Rees later labelled 'bandit country', the battalion would lose four of its own men on Armagh's roads, plus two soldiers of 17th/21st Royal Lancers and a Royal Engineer Search Advisor. Private Steven Norris and Lance Corporal Terence Brown died when their Land Rover was blown up by a 300lb (137kg) mine hidden under a culvert in Tullyogallaghan on 7 April 1973. Another soldier serving with 2 Para at the time recalls how one of his abiding memories of the tour was the blood-soaked stretchers being washed down in the shower block at Bessbrook Mill, one of the Army's key bases in the area.

In another incident four weeks later Company Sergeant Major Ron Vines of 2 Para was killed when a pressure-pad he stepped on initiated a landmine explosion. The device's command wire led across the border near Moybane, south-east of Crossmaglen. As Sergeant Major Vines walked over to a roadside wall, the 400lb (181kg) IRA bomb detonated, killing him instantly. His wife later said that she 'didn't even have a body to bury'. In the follow-up operation mounted by the Army in the aftermath of the explosion two other

soldiers, Troopers Terence Williams and John Gibbons of 17th/21st Royal Lancers, were blown up by a secondary device on the same spot where Company Sergeant-Major Vines had died. An Army spokesman later said that the mood of the local civilian population in South Armagh had been 'extremely hostile'. Support for the IRA was high in republican areas. As one former IRA volunteer recalled while speaking to the author, 'you cannot run a guerrilla campaign without the support of the community'.

As the conflict progressed the Army became better at countering IRA anti-personnel devices. Government scientists developed electronic counter-measures (ECM), which would afford soldiers deployed on patrol a degree

A soldier was killed when the Provisional IRA detonated a 400lb roadside bomb in Crossmaglen, South Armagh, in October 1975. Such attacks spurred on the development of electronic counter-measures. (Keystone Press / Alamy Stock Photo)

of force protection. In an interview with the author, one seasoned veteran of Operation *Banner* recalled how his life 'was saved on more than one occasion' by the 'ECM bubble'. As the Army's 'lessons-learned' pamphlet *Military Operations in Northern Ireland* makes clear, this 'situation rapidly evolved into a continuous struggle between development and counter'.

The implementation of a rigorous pre-deployment training package delivered by the Northern Ireland Training and Advisory Team (NITAT) to all units in the United Kingdom and Germany also served to hone the Army's tactical skills and drills. In an interview with the author, one former UDR officer who served on the Directing Staff at NITAT in Sennelager, Germany, pointed out that troops were put through rigorous training before they arrived 'in theatre' for operations, as 'the more you could plant those wee seeds the better they were prepared'. Debriefs were especially important because soldiers soon became accustomed to the intelligence picture and how their role was vital in the overall security situation. When they eventually deployed to the province, units underwent further training in counter-IED tactics, advanced search techniques, and the application of ROE.[*]

Northern Ireland, therefore, presented a unique soldiering environment. It demanded not only the confident application of infantry skills, such as proficiency in weapons-handling techniques and fieldcraft, but also a high level of Internal Security drills. The province's terrain was variable and ranged from the 303 miles of (largely rural) border separating north and south to the tight alleyways of inner-city Belfast. Peter Morton, a former Commanding Officer of 3 Para, explained how 'the fighting machine [was] broken up into individuals and small teams who can think and

---

[*]   In order to counter 'skills fade' the Army also introduced 'roulement' battalions that would deploy for pre-defined periods of time of several months in high-intensity areas, such as West Belfast, and 'resident' battalions that would move their headquarters and sub-units to Northern Ireland with their families for longer tours of up to two years.

operate sensitively, intelligently and always within the law no matter how provocative or frightening the situation they find themselves'. As the threat from the IRA began to change, the Army adapted to meet the challenge, including working to integrate more closely with RUC officers and their priorities on the ground. Joint military–police operations would begin to slowly improve in the late 1970s.

Combatting terrorism

Ever since the mid-1970s the Labour government in London had sought to explore possible exit strategies from Northern Ireland. Government officials began to look for ways to bolster the profile of the RUC and the locally recruited UDR, by now the British Army's largest infantry regiment, under a strategy of 'Ulsterization'. This policy of handing over responsibility for security matters to local indigenous Security Forces had characterized Britain's approach to counter-insurgency and counter-terrorist operations throughout the post-war period. During the Mau Mau Emergency in Kenya in the 1950s Britain opted for 'Africanization', in which the colonial government backed up by British troops formed, equipped and trained 'Home Guard' units to protect vulnerable villages from attack. In the 1960s, during the Aden Emergency, British forces again mentored Federation troops under the guiding principle of 'Arabization', as Aden made the transition towards independence.

Established in 1970 as an instrument to counter terrorism in the province, the UDR was deemed to be invaluable because its members lived and worked in the areas where they soldiered and could thus draw on their excellent local knowledge. However, unlike the 'B' Specials, the UDR was born out of the political attempts to make military back-up more indigenous. While it was thought that the UDR would attract sufficient numbers of Catholics, this hope soon proved ill-founded for a variety of reasons, not least because the

IRA intimidated many Catholics into leaving its ranks. Formed largely along British military lines, the UDR was fortunate to be able to call upon the professionalism of its Permanent Staff Instructors, many of whom had transferred into or were on attachment from the regular British Army regiments.

In setting up a ministerial committee to examine security policy, Northern Ireland Secretary of State Merlyn Rees said that it should seek

> …[t]o examine the action and resources required for the next few years to maintain law and order in Northern Ireland, including how best to achieve the primacy of the Police; the size and role of locally recruited forces; and the progressive reduction of the Army as soon as is practicable.

The government came to believe that scaling back the regular Army's role in favour of raising the RUC's profile, with the UDR in support when required, was the right course of action.

The UDR soon became experts in the tactical side of the campaign and their numbers were increased as regular troops were withdrawn for duties elsewhere. At the time of Operation *Motorman* in July 1972 there were approximately 19 units on the Army's Order of Battle in Northern Ireland, the equivalent of 21,000 troops. That figure declined to 15 units in 1975 and 13 in 1979, with some 13,600 troops stationed in the province by the end of the decade.

Table 3. Security Forces Strength, 1969–98					
Year	Regular	UDR/ RIR	Army Total	RUC Total	Total
1969	2,700	0	2,700	3,500	6,200
1970	6,300	2,292	8,592	3,750	12,342
1971	7,800	4,044	11,844	4,083	15,927

1972	14,300	8,476	22,776	4,273	27,049
1973	16,900	8,443	25,343	4,421	29,764
1974	16,200	7,815	24,015	4,563	28,578
1975	15,000	7,692	22,692	4,902	27,594
1976	15,500	7,645	23,145	5,253	28,398
1977	14,300	7,651	21,951	5,692	27,643
1978	14,400	7,970	22,370	6,110	28,480
1979	13,600	7,518	21,118	6,614	27,732
1980	11,900	7,376	19,276	6,935	26,211
1981	11,600	7,470	19,070	7,334	26,404
1982	10,900	7,111	18,011	7,717	25,728
1983	10,200	6,925	17,125	8,003	25,128
1984	10,000	6,468	16,468	8,127	24,595
1985	9,700	6,494	16,194	8,259	24,453
1986	10,500	6,408	16,908	8,234	25,142
1987	11,400	6,531	17,931	8,236	26,167
1988	11,200	6,393	17,593	8,231	25,824
1989	11,200	6,230	17,430	8,259	25,689
1990	10,500	6,043	16,543	8,243	24,786
1991	10,500	6,276	16,776	8,222	24,998
1992	12,000	5,417	17,417	8,483	25,900
1993	13,000	5,412	18,412	8,470	26,882
1994	11,759	5,241	17,000	8,469	25,469
1995	12,019	5,170	17,189	8,499	25,688
1996	11,815	4,855	16,670	8,424	25,094
1997	12,477	4,757	17,234	8,430	25,664
1998	12,346	4,598	16,944	8,495	25,439

The reduction in the numbers of regular troops, however, masked another important change in the operational tempo of the Army's role in Northern Ireland. In response to the sectarian murders of ten Protestant workmen near Kingsmill, South Armagh, on 5 January 1976, Prime Minister Harold Wilson authorized the deployment of the SAS to the area. The unit's role was primarily reconnaissance and the interdiction of IRA members as they staged attacks on Security Forces.

Perhaps anticipating the steady build-up of pressure from Special Forces, the Provisional IRA took the decision in November 1976 to restructure its organization along cellular lines and prepare for a 'long war'. The IRA formed a semi-autonomous Northern Command operational structure, which ensured it could exert maximum pressure on the Security Forces inside Northern Ireland, rather than completing tasks issued to it directly from a General Headquarters in Dublin. This led inevitably to a resurgent republican threat, making a permanent drawdown of regular troops deployed on Operation *Banner* unlikely. Moreover, there is evidence to suggest that an upsurge in IRA attacks in West Belfast had taken the Army by surprise, a jolt that, as one intelligence report candidly revealed, 'must be seen as further evidence of our lack of tactical intelligence in West Belfast'.

By the mid-1970s the security picture in places like West Belfast became more complicated. The IRA was coming under increasing pressure to defend the nationalist community who were suffering from sustained attack by sectarian killers within the UVF and UDA. Tit-for-tat bombings and shootings between loyalists and republicans had been a common feature of the Troubles for several years. Attacks on pubs and social clubs were commonplace. Deep-seated residential segregation made it relatively straightforward for rival groups to attack their perceived enemies without endangering those 'on their side'. Loyalists were cruder in their targeting than republicans, in large part because, as they argued, the IRA 'did not wear a uniform'. The emergence of the 'Shankill Butchers' gang, a unit within the West Belfast UVF, further increased the general feeling of fear and anxiety within the nationalist community. The gang earned its nickname for killing its victims, mainly Catholic but also some Protestants, by abducting, torturing and then killing them with knives stolen from a butcher's shop. Although loyalist paramilitaries did not possess the same degree of technical sophistication that marked out the Provisional IRA as a deadly terrorist organization, this made them no less dangerous. The mid-1970s marked the high water mark of sectarian killings, a reality not lost on British politicians in London.

After Harold Wilson's resignation in March 1976, his successor as prime minister, James Callaghan, replaced Merlyn Rees as secretary of state for Northern Ireland with Roy Mason. A tough-talking Yorkshireman and former miner who had been a leading trade unionist, Mason had served as defence secretary before taking up his new post at the Northern Ireland Office (NIO).

An Ulster Defence Association parade in June 1972. The UDA began as a vigilante movement in Belfast, spreading across Northern Ireland. At its peak, it had over 40,000 members. (Photo by David Lomax/ Keystone/Hulton Archive/Getty Images)

The tough-talking former miner Roy Mason served as Labour's Defence Secretary in 1974–76 and as Northern Ireland Secretary in 1976–79. He was an implacable opponent of the Provisional IRA. (Photo by Central Press/Hulton Archive/Getty Images)

Mason was a staunch opponent of terrorism, harbouring a particular dislike for the Provisional IRA. Unlike his predecessors, Mason took a hard-line attitude towards violence and his tenure as Northern Ireland Secretary was marked by an increase in Special Forces operations. As Mason made clear in a public statement in May 1977, 'The number of special security forces such as the SAS had been substantially increased and this trend would continue'. In a letter to his successor at the Ministry of Defence, Fred Mulley, Mason wrote:

> We have been aware for some time of the tremendous and lasting boost for public morale which followed the posting of an SAS Squadron to South Armagh sixteen months ago. It says a great deal for the SAS Regiment's reputation for professional skill in the counter-terrorist role that ever since their arrival, there have been calls for their operations to be extended and their number increased.

NORTH
CHANNEL

N

IRISH
SEA

LOUGH
FOYLE

○ Coleraine

○Ballykelly

Ballymoney

8 ⊠

Derry/
Londonderry

○Garvagh

○Ballymena

Larne

● Brigade
headquarters
locations

○Strabane

Magherafelt○

Antrim

Carrickfergus

Holywood

○Castlederg

Cookstown○

LOUGH
NEAGH

Belfast

Newtownards

DONEGAL
BAY

Omagh

Dungannon

Ladas Drive

39 ⊠

Lisburn●

Carryduff

○St Angelo

Aughnacloy

8 ⊠

3 ⊠

● Lurgan
(1972–76)

Enniskillen○

Clogher

3 ⊠

Portadown
(1976–81)

○Lisnaskea

○Lisnaskea

Armagh
(1988–2004)

Glenanne

Rathfriland

Ballykinler

20 miles

40 km

○Kilkeel

Noting the success of the Army's role in the covert war against the IRA, Mason asked Mulley 'whether more could be done' to ensure 'a better success rate' and 'to give extra credence to our claim that the Army's expertise in dealing with terrorists continues to grow'. Mason's correspondence with Mulley on clandestine operations demonstrated the British government's understanding of the changing character of the terrorist threat. In Mason's words: '[T]he problem has ceased to be one of large confrontations with rioters and is one of identifying and tracing and finding evidence against small groups of terrorists'. To that end Mason became an enthusiastic supporter of the need for further covert action.

One of those conducting this secret war against the IRA was Captain Robert Nairac. A colourful if somewhat controversial figure, Nairac was a Liaison Officer between Special Forces and the RUC Special Branch. One of those who served alongside Nairac told the author that he 'had a great personality and made friends easily with the result that he was an excellent Liaison Officer'. On an undercover mission to apparently meet a contact at the Three Steps pub in Drumintee, Nairac was badly beaten and abducted by the IRA. One of the IRA men who tortured and killed Nairac later admitted, 'I shot the British Captain. He never told us anything. He was a great soldier.' In February 1979 Nairac was posthumously awarded the George Cross, Britain's second-highest award for gallantry. Part of his citation read:

> Captain Nairac served for four tours of duty in Northern Ireland totalling twenty-eight months. During the whole of this time he made an outstanding personal contribution: his quick analytical brain, resourcefulness, physical stamina and above all his courage and dedication inspired admiration in everyone who knew him.

The difficulty in deciphering exactly what Nairac was doing in Northern Ireland during his four tours or on the night he died illustrates how covert action was undertaken on a 'need-to-know' basis. As another veteran of Operation *Banner*, General Sir Mike Jackson, explained in his memoirs:

> Intelligence and the response to it were handled on a very tight, need-to-know basis. Even when I was a brigade commander, I would not necessarily be in the loop. There would be a directive that uniformed troops were to keep out of a particular area between this time and that time because it had been 'sanitized' for a particular operation. I didn't always know what was going on, but I didn't always need to know.

The Army's covert war in the late 1970s enjoyed only mixed success. Military intelligence had certainly improved its collection capabilities while also strengthening its cooperation with other intelligence agencies, though it still had a long way to go.

Provisional IRA chiefs like Martin McGuinness became advocates for a new military strategy that

Robert Nairac was a Troop Leader in the Special Reconnaissance Unit, serving as a Liaison Officer when he was abducted and murdered by the Provisional IRA on 15 May 1977. (Sandhurst Collection)

prioritized using violence for quick propaganda wins. One prime target for the IRA were members of the locally recruited UDR. UDR soldiers were routinely targeted when they were off duty. For republicans these 'soft targets' were much easier to eliminate because of the likelihood that they would be caught off-guard and unarmed.

On 8 October 1977 Private Margaret Hearst, a part-time member of 2 UDR, was shot dead while sleeping in a caravan beside her parents' home near

Middletown in County Armagh. Females had been admitted into the UDR from 1973 and it was Army policy for servicewomen to be unarmed, a stance that remained unchanged until the 1990s. A gunman broke into Hearst's parents' home, terrorized her aunt and two young brothers, and then entered the caravan in which she and her three-year-old daughter were sleeping. The 16-year-old IRA gunman fired ten or 11 shots at Private Hearst from an Armalite rifle, killing her instantly, but narrowly missing her young daughter. The gunman and his accomplices then fled the scene to the 'safe haven' of the Irish Republic, where they attended a dance in Monaghan. In the follow-up operation the murder weapon was uncovered in a hedgerow approximately 550 yards south of the Hearsts' home. Private Hearst was the first 'Greenfinch' (female member of the UDR) to be killed while off duty; her murder, which was claimed by the IRA, was widely condemned.

Tragedy struck the Hearst family again in September 1980 when Private Hearst's father, Ross, was abducted and shot dead by the IRA. His 'crime', said the IRA, was to admit, during torture, that he had supplied information to the Security Forces. Not only was the organization targeting off-duty UDR soldiers, but it had now sunk to a new low by assassinating members of the wider Protestant community. Actions like these exposed the sectarian nature of Provisional IRA violence, particularly in rural areas.

The IRA preferred to attack off-duty UDR personnel principally because their targets lived and worked in the communities they served, and were therefore vulnerable. UDR personnel – both full- and part-time – had to hide their profession for security reasons and entered into a routine of checking under cars and varying routes to and from their places of work and bases, as well as taking security measures to protect themselves and their families from attack. Of the 204 UDR and Royal Irish (Home Service Force) soldiers murdered, 162 (or 79 per cent) were killed off duty, with some 60 ex-UDR members killed by republicans.

In an interview with the author one former UDR soldier from the Derry/Londonderry area recalled how he 'ended up thinking like a terrorist in order to stay alive'. Opportunities for a social life were minimal, and the personal security precautions were essential. One vignette sums up the atmosphere neatly:

> I was followed home from work one night. I immediately realized that I was being followed. After speeding up to 94 miles per hour I slammed on the brakes. The hunter became the hunted. I followed suit but lost them. Running into a police checkpoint I then informed them of the car registration number. It later transpired that four prominent members of the IRA were out to kill me. They were dressed head-to-toe in khaki jackets.

Many UDR soldiers automatically assumed that IRA volunteers were out for a kill. The UDR soldier interviewed by the author recalled being asked on one occasion whether he would move house, to which he replied that they would track him down wherever he

The UDR was at one time the largest regiment in the British Army, established in 1970. Its members lived in the community and were subject to daily threat from terrorists. (Photo by Alex Bowie/Getty Images)

went – and, besides, had the IRA decided to attack his home, it was 'him or me': 'If they came to the house they would have found themselves in a battle' but they were 'fucking cowards'. In his words, 'the IRA never looked their victims in the eye … except for the team led by [South Derry INLA leader Dominic McGlinchey] who made a point of doing that'.

As the former UDR soldier went on to say, 'I lost numerous friends. How did I feel? Anger when a colleague was murdered. You wanted to seek revenge, but professionalism kicked in. Instinct kicked in and you got on with the job.' He saw himself very much as 'the hunted'. The terrorists knew every move he made and he was engaged in a 'war of survival' on a daily basis. The primary weapon employed by the IRA on soft targets was the under-car booby-trap bomb. 'If you could counter their defences they observed you from a distance and a secondary attack – a shoot – was mounted.' The IRA, however, relied on the patterns set by Security Forces personnel, whether on or off duty. 'Some journeys to and from work, such as a six-mile trip, which would take ten minutes in a normal society took half an hour. I wasn't driving directly to work and when I left work I never took the same route home.' Even so, the unpredictability of IRA attacks and the sophistication of their intelligence, targeting and killing capabilities made the IRA a versatile opponent.

The IRA's objective of attacking soft targets was further illustrated when they detonated a bomb under the family car of off-duty UDR member William Gordon, killing him and his ten-year-old daughter Lesley outside their home in Maghera, County Derry/Londonderry, on 8 February 1978. His wife was waving goodbye with the couple's baby in her arms when the bomb exploded. The Gordons' seven-year-old son Richard, who was in the back seat at the time, was blown out of the car and onto the footpath. One eyewitness said that most of the car ended up on the roof of a house 60 yards away. Speaking in the wake of the attack and a few days after the La Mon Hotel atrocity, which claimed the lives of 12 Protestants, Shadow Northern Ireland Secretary Airey

Neave expressed the view that 'the Special Air Service on our side could play a big role here'. Within a year Neave was himself assassinated by the INLA when he was blown up by an under-car booby trap bomb as he drove out of the House of Commons car park.

The IRA successfully assassinated other high-profile targets too. On 27 August 1979 the organization murdered Lord Louis Mountbatten, the Queen's cousin, who was taking his pleasure boat out of the harbour at Mullaghmore, County Sligo, in the Irish Republic, when the IRA detonated a remote-control bomb. Lord Mountbatten's murder sent shockwaves through the British establishment. Two young boys, aged 14 and 15, one of them Lord Mountbatten's grandson, were also killed in the explosion.

Lord Mountbatten pictured here with his cousin, Queen Elizabeth II. Mountbatten was Chief of the Defence Staff in 1959–65. He was assassinated by the Provisional IRA on 27 August 1979. (Photo by Fox Photos/Hulton Archive/Getty Images)

Eighteen soldiers lost their lives in a twin remote-control bomb attack when their vehicle convoy passed close to the Irish border on 27 August 1979. (Pacemaker Press International)

Civilians caught up in such attacks were regarded by the IRA and its apologists as 'collateral damage'.

Later that day the IRA targeted a convoy of soldiers transiting from one security forces base to another. Sixteen members of the Parachute Regiment's second battalion lost their lives along with another two soldiers from the Queen's Own Highlanders. The co-ordinated attack near Warrenpoint, County Down, demonstrated that the IRA could also execute bigger and more sophisticated operations.

Intelligence-led operations

Attacks on the Security Forces became much more frequent in the early 1980s. The use of heavier-calibre weapons in the late 1970s alarmed government officials and military commanders. Roy Mason had earlier warned that the IRA had even managed to smuggle in some M60 machine guns from the United States. Because of what he called 'their diminishing resources', Mason believed the IRA's aim was 'to find something

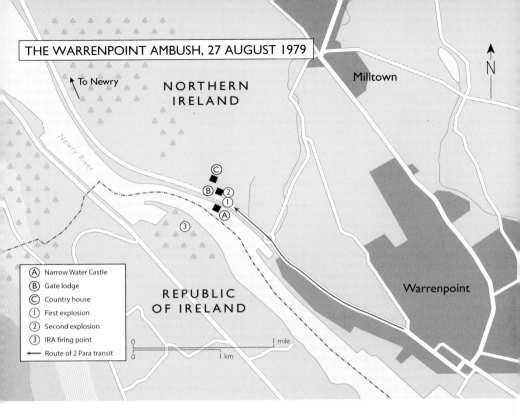

To Newry

NORTHERN
IRELAND

Milltown

N

Newry River

Ⓒ
Ⓑ ②
①
Ⓐ

③

Ⓐ Narrow Water Castle
Ⓑ Gate lodge
Ⓒ Country house
① First explosion
② Second explosion
③ IRA firing point
◄— Route of 2 Para transit

REPUBLIC
OF IRELAND

Warrenpoint

0 _____ 1 mile
0 _____ 1 km

different and the M60 is a new dimension'. The SAS was
now tasked to recover these weapons. In one incident
on 2 May 1980, an IRA ASU (Active Service Unit, the
nomenclature adopted when the IRA switched to a more
tightly organized cellular unit structure) opened fire with
an M60 on an eight-man SAS team as they stormed a
house on the Antrim Road in North Belfast. The burst
of fire killed the team leader, Captain Richard Herbert
Westmacott, instantly. The IRA unit had pre-planned
the operation at a variety of different locations across
the city, unaware of the presence of an informer in their
ranks. Intelligence was passed on to the Tasking and Co-
ordination Group, the operational hub of the Security
Forces based at the RUC's police station in Castlereagh,
and the SAS was allocated the mission of neutralizing
what became known as the 'M60 gang'. Owing to
a map-reading error the SAS team entered the wrong
house, with the terrorists holed up next door, a mistake
which very nearly cost the lives of more soldiers.

Margaret Thatcher was nicknamed 'The Iron Lady' for her steely resolve on defence- and security-related matters. Mrs Thatcher endorsed a more coercive response to terrorism in Northern Ireland during 1979–90. (Bettmann/Getty Images)

Local New Lodge man Joe Doherty and another member of the ASU had been trained as snipers and knew the routine of Army patrols in the area well. The IRA's M60 gang had a fearsome reputation and was equipped with an assortment of other weapons, including a Heckler & Koch submachine gun and FAL self-loading rifles, as well as several handguns. The gang's *modus operandi* had been to ambush Security Forces patrols as they passed through republican areas. The following year seven IRA men were charged with the SAS officer's murder, only for two of them to escape from custody.

The M60 was again used by the IRA on 16 July 1981, when 18 soldiers of 1st Battalion, The Royal

Green Jackets (1 RGJ), on a four-month emergency tour were dropped off on a covert reconnaissance mission at Glassdrummond, between Crossmaglen and Forkhill. Within a matter of hours, the close-observation platoon's position had been compromised by locals, who then alerted the IRA. Moments later an IRA ASU opened fire from across the border. The van used to extract the British soldiers was hit by 150 bullets from an assortment of weapons, including an M60, four Armalite rifles and a .303 rifle. Lance Corporal Gavin Dean was shot dead and two of his comrades wounded.

Only a few weeks before, on 19 May 1981, 1 RGJ had lost four riflemen and an attached driver from the Royal Corps of Transport in a massive landmine strike. Experts later said that a 1,000lb (454kg) bomb had totally obliterated the Saracen armoured car. Tragedy was not to end there for the regiment, however, as a roadside bomb claimed the lives of three more riflemen on 23 March 1982, a couple of weeks into their two-year

The Provisional IRA bombed the Queen's Life Guard as they made their way through Hyde Park on 20 July 1982. Four soldiers and seven horses died in the attack. (Photo by © Hulton-Deutsch Collection/CORBIS/ Corbis via Getty Images)

A mural to Bobby Sands, the leader of the Provisional IRA's hunger strike in the Maze prison in 1981. He died after refusing food for 66 days. (Edwards Collection)

residential tour. And in one of the most sickening attacks of the Troubles, four soldiers from the Household Cavalry, the Queen's official bodyguard, were killed instantly when a car bomb exploded as they made their way through Hyde Park to their duties in Whitehall. A second bomb placed under the bandstand in Regent's Park was detonated two hours later, claiming the lives of seven bandsmen from the Royal Green Jackets who were playing a lunchtime concert.

What made the mood of this period particularly intense was that military operations were conducted against the backdrop of a republican hunger strike in the Maze prison over a dispute with the authorities. Eventually, ten IRA and INLA prisoners were to die, including Bobby Sands, who had been elected to Westminster as an MP for Fermanagh and South Tyrone. Sands died on 5 May 1981 after refusing food for 66 days. Unsurprisingly, violence escalated in the wake of the hunger strikes. It led to a polarization between the two communities, and, interestingly, also to a groundswell in popular support for the dead republicans, which in turn prompted an upsurge in Sinn Féin's electoral fortunes. The IRA increased its operations against the Army and in one particularly shocking incident five soldiers were blown up and killed in a mine-strike against their armoured personnel carrier near Omagh, County Tyrone.

Republican terrorists also returned to targeting off-duty soldiers. On 6 December 1982, a devastating no-warning bomb attack on the Droppin' Well pub in Ballykelly, close to Shackleton Barracks, killed 11 soldiers and six civilians. The INLA later admitted responsibility. Meanwhile, the IRA had renewed its campaign against the locally recruited UDR, abducting off-duty personnel before torturing and then shooting them. On 17 October 1982, Sergeant Thomas Cochrane, an off-duty UDR soldier, was travelling home from his civilian job at Glennane linen mill near Markethill, South Armagh, when IRA members felled him from his motorcycle, bundled him into a car and took him away to torture him. The organization released a statement saying he was being held for 'interrogation because of his crimes against the Nationalist community'. The IRA hoped to gain valuable intelligence about his comrades in the UDR; knowing that he was going to be killed, however, Cochrane gave his captors nothing. The IRA murdered him and dumped his body in Lislea, Armagh, five days after his abduction, proving

Patrick Magee, a Provisional IRA bombmaker, was tasked with assassinating Margaret Thatcher as she attended the Conservative Party conference in Brighton in 1984. She survived. Five people were killed and 31 injured. (Photo by Terry Fincher/The Fincher Files/Popperfoto via Getty Images)

Provisional IRA members pictured along the Irish border in August 1986. One member is carrying an Armalite, a prized weapon smuggled to the IRA from supporters in the United States. (Photo by Kaveh Kazemi/Getty Images)

yet again, in Ed Moloney's words, that 'targeting members of the … [UDR] for death was an integral part of IRA strategy'.

Most UDR members and their families remained hyper-vigilant as a result, many going on to suffer significant post-traumatic stress from years living under threat of death at the hands of IRA gunmen. 'When off-duty soldiers were kidnapped they were taken to killing houses where they were beaten and horrifically mutilated,' recalled one former UDR soldier. 'That is the reality. And a bomb was placed under the body for Security Forces personnel as a "come on".'

One example of a 'come on' was the cold-blooded murder of a 62-year-old civilian chief instructor employed at Magilligan Prison. Leslie Jarvis, who attended night classes at Magee College, was shot dead as he sat in his car outside the college on 23 March 1987. His body was then booby-trapped and left for unsuspecting members of the Security Forces; the device exploded a short time later, killing two policemen who were investigating the shooting.

In a bid to reduce the IRA's capacity for mounting attacks on Security Forces personnel, the Army's Special Forces units increasingly came to the forefront in the 1980s. As journalist Mark Urban has observed, 'Throughout the ten years which followed [from 1976], the importance of the "Green Army" – groups of uniformed regular soldiers – in confronting terrorism fell as the role of undercover forces grew.' The undercover war was now overtaking the overt military presence as the SAS, Military Intelligence and other security agencies intensified their covert operations against republican and

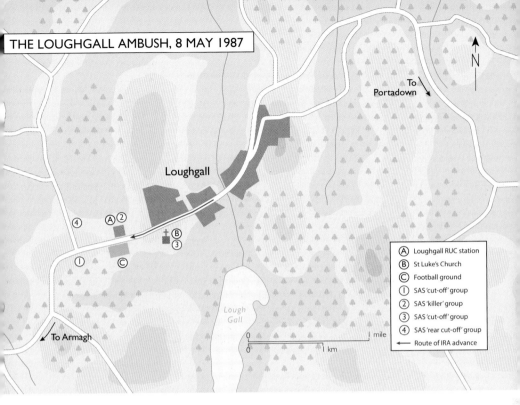

Loughgall

To Portadown

N

To Armagh

Lough Gall

A Loughgall RUC station
B St Luke's Church
C Football ground
1 SAS 'cut-off' group
2 SAS 'killer' group
3 SAS 'cut-off' group
4 SAS 'rear cut-off' group
← Route of IRA advance

0 ————————— 1 mile
0 ————————— 1 km

loyalist terrorists. In statistical terms, over 30 Provisional IRA members and two INLA members had been killed and many more arrested by undercover soldiers between 1976 and 1987. Some journalists have claimed that this high attrition rate was made possible only because Security Forces intelligence 'had been excellent'. Intelligence-gathering was the lifeblood of Security Forces operations throughout Operation *Banner*. One former undercover soldier told the author that 'the covert war was a bigger battle than the overt war'.

On 8 May 1987 eight members of the Provisional IRA's East Tyrone brigade were cut down in a hail of SAS bullets as they attempted to attack an RUC station in the sleepy County Armagh village of Loughgall. A 24-strong SAS team had been assembled in Mahon Road Barracks, Portadown, on the evening before the shooting. Outnumbering the IRA by three to one they split up into a 'killer group' and three 'cut-off groups', each taking up position to ambush the terrorists. The

An eight-strong IRA squad led by Patrick Kelly launched a bomb and gun attack on Loughgall RUC station on 8 May 1987. They were ambushed by the SAS. (Pacemaker Press International)

IRA had earlier hijacked a mechanical digger; loading a 200lb (91kg) bomb into its bucket, three of the terrorists travelled in its cab and five others in a blue Toyota HiAce van. The van reached Loughgall at 1915 hours, passing the church and driving down the hill to the station before going back up. After making sure the coast was clear it returned, closely followed by the mechanical digger. At about 1920 hours the van came to a halt in front of the station. The IRA men in the van dismounted and opened fire with their automatic weapons. At the same time the digger crashed into the wall and the IRA men on board lit the fuse, at which point the SAS ambush was sprung. Over 1,500 rounds were fired by the SAS soldiers and RUC Special Branch officers who were accompanying them.

This was not the first time the IRA had attacked RUC stations. On 28 February 1985 the IRA had mortared Newry RUC station, killing nine police officers, the largest single loss of life incurred by the RUC in the Troubles. In May the same year the IRA blew up a mobile police patrol, killing four officers, and on 7 December it launched an attack on Ballygawley RUC barracks, killing two policemen. This last attack was much more audacious and involved IRA volunteers raking the police station with gunfire and then blowing it up. It was a tactic repeated again on 11 August 1986, when the IRA destroyed the RUC station at the Birches, County Tyrone.

In an oration at the graveside of the eight dead IRA volunteers, Gerry Adams said that Loughgall would become 'a tombstone for British policy in Ireland and a bloody milestone in the struggle for freedom, justice and peace'. Strategically, though, the IRA was staring defeat in the face. In the 1980s and 1990s nine out of every ten operations were aborted or failed. By now Security Forces intelligence operations were scoring huge successes.

Perhaps one of the most controversial aspects of the Security Forces' secret war against the IRA and loyalist paramilitaries was their ability to penetrate terrorist organizations with what the military called Human Intelligence (HUMINT) sources and what the RUC called two-legged agents. The number of informants and agents, known more commonly in paramilitary circles as 'touts', operating at any one time is difficult to quantify. Former Special Branch officer William Matchett has estimated that around 15 key agents were working within the Provisional IRA at any one time. The IRA certainly believed informers were a problem for it is said to have killed 70 suspected informers during its long campaign. Some of the most experienced journalists to cover the IRA's armed campaign have also alleged that informers were responsible for compromising several of the IRA's missions in the late 1980s, including those carried out by its East Tyrone squad, which had killed several hundred people during the Troubles, although it had itself lost a total of 53 volunteers, of whom just over half – 28 – were killed in the five years after 1987.

Running alongside the corrosive effects of HUMINT was the escalating violence of loyalist paramilitaries. In part this was attributable to a more honed intelligence-gathering capability and the influx of new weaponry smuggled in from South Africa, which permitted the UVF and UDA to enhance the sophistication of their operations.

The shift from a random sectarian campaign of violence to a more focused and co-ordinated effort to assassinate individual republicans led some unionist politicians to suggest that the loyalists were having an effect on the IRA. Nationalist politicians offered another reason for the successes of loyalist paramilitaries: collusion.

In response to allegations of collusion between some elements of the Security Forces and terrorist groups, Margaret Thatcher's Conservative government appointed Sir John Stephens, the former Metropolitan Police Commissioner, to undertake an investigation into the UFF murders of a Catholic, Patrick Finucane, and a Protestant, Brian Adam Lambert. But so protracted was the process that his findings and recommendations for the period 1987–2003 were published only in April 2003. Towards the end of his report, Stephens concluded that

> … there was collusion in both murders and the circumstances surrounding them. Collusion is evidenced

Two soldiers from the King's Own Scottish Borderers died when a dozen IRA terrorists attacked the checkpoint in Derryard between Fivemiletown and Rosslea in County Fermanagh on 13 December 1989. (Pacemaker Press International)

in many ways. This ranges from the wilful failure to keep records, the absence of accountability, the withholding of intelligence and evidence, through to the extreme of agents being involved in murder.

Controversy still surrounds these killings and other incidents in the 'dirty war' and continues to dominate republican thinking on the legacy of the Troubles.

Between 1987 and 1989 the RUC dealt with over 3,000 terrorist-related incidents, of which 261 were Troubles-related deaths. The Provisional IRA had by now been developing more deadly techniques. On 24 October 1990 it unveiled a deadly new tactic, when it carried out a 1,000lb (454kg) proxy bomb attack on the Coshquin PVCP (Permanent Vehicle Checkpoint).* Five soldiers from 1st Battalion, The King's Regiment, and a civilian (the driver of the van carrying the bomb) were killed. The civilian, Patrick 'Patsy' Gillespie, had worked in the canteen of a local Security Forces base. His family was taken hostage and held at gunpoint, while he was ordered to drive the van and its deadly cargo to the target.

By the early 1990s Ulsterization was becoming a reality. The UDR had become a much more professional military organization. As one former UDR officer recalled, 'the UDR grew from being a part-time, bunch of colonials into a more professional organization'. It had by now been given further operational responsibilities as the numbers of regular troops began to drop off, particularly as there were now pressures coming from the 1990 'Options for Change' defence review and overseas commitments in the Gulf. In the defence review a number of infantry regiments were amalgamated, including the UDR and the regular battalions of the Royal Irish Rangers, leading to the formation of the Royal Irish Regiment in 1992.

* PVCPs gave troops the flexibility to mount a permanent presence around their patrol bases and observation posts dotted along the border. Many of the Army's border bases were 'supersangars', 65ft-high watchtowers erected as surveillance and listening posts.

The political and military pressure exerted on the IRA forced the organization to switch its attention to more high-profile targets on the British mainland. In February 1991 the IRA launched an audacious mortar attack on No. 10 Downing Street. A series of co-ordinated attacks on the London Stock Exchange applied further pressure, leading unionist politician Robert McCartney to remark that 'a bomb in London is worth 100 in Belfast'. These attacks demonstrated how the IRA's campaign was increasing in intensity. A shipment of IRA arms destined for Belfast was intercepted in 1994; however, there were suggestions that more than three-quarters of the consignment had successfully reached its destination.

While there was a dip in the number of operations mounted by the IRA, loyalist violence continued unabated. The brutal sectarian killings of four workmen in Castlerock on 25 March 1993 and the indiscriminate attack on the Rising Sun bar in Greysteel, near Derry/ Londonderry City, on 30 October that year were particularly shocking. The Greysteel massacre was exceptionally callous, with UFF gunman Torrens Knight and his accomplice heard shouting 'trick or treat' before opening fire, spraying the packed bar with over 30 bullets. Some 200 people had been in the bar that evening and it was a miracle that the attack claimed only eight victims. The Greysteel attack was mounted in retaliation for the IRA bombing of Frizzel's fish-and-chip shop on the Shankill Road a few days earlier, which claimed the lives of nine civilians. The IRA volunteer responsible, Thomas Begley, also died as the bomb he was transporting blew up prematurely. Issuing a statement to the media shortly afterwards, the IRA claimed that the operation was intended to target a UFF meeting in an upstairs office. Violence continued steadily into 1994, as the IRA targeted Heathrow Airport on several occasions in March. Meanwhile the group also undertook a co-ordinated assassination campaign against loyalist paramilitaries. On all fronts the violence continued unchecked with little prospect of an end in sight.

THE WORLD AROUND WAR
A place apart?

Northern Ireland is a deeply divided society, and one which finds echoes around the world. Like rival Greek and Turkish Cypriots in the eastern Mediterranean or the Israelis and Palestinians in the Middle East, Protestant unionists and Catholic nationalists share one land, but are separated by religion, history and culture. Reinforcing the conflict are the overlapping – albeit divergent – national identities held by the two communities. Most Protestants regard themselves as British and wish to maintain the union with Great Britain, while most Catholics wish to jettison these ties, abolish partition and unite Ireland. The strong bond between local communities and neighbouring states is common throughout Europe and the rest of the world, and it is echoed in much of the wall art decorating urban areas across Northern Ireland. In many ways one of the most telling aspects of the Troubles is the empathy the main parties to the conflict have with those undergoing similar trials and tribulations elsewhere.

The international dimension has been a constant feature of the Troubles ever since they exploded onto the streets in the late 1960s. Indeed, for the outside world the clashes between police, soldiers and street protestors remain the conflict's defining images. Scenes of widespread disorder, baton charges by the Security

Forces, masked gunmen and rioters, homes reduced to rubble, and streets awash with water-cannon spray and littered with smashed glass and bricks were common features of other deeply divided societies. What made the Troubles in Ulster unique, however, was the way in which the violence was portrayed as indelibly ethnic or tribal, and somewhat out of sync with the wider Cold War confrontation between West and East. This caricature of Northern Ireland being 'a place apart' has since been challenged, particularly as ethnic conflict exploded after the fall of the Iron Curtain and end of the Cold War.

The other conflicts helped to fire up the imagination of many student radicals and civil rights activists. Interestingly, the Troubles erupted at a time when feelings in Northern Ireland were already running high, inflamed by global issues such as segregation in the American Deep South and the United States' intervention in Vietnam. In the US, armed militias like the Black Panthers took advantage of the civil disorder and could frequently be seen flanking those calling for the withdrawal of troops from south-east Asia, as well as those marching in solidarity with the North Vietnamese-sponsored insurgent groups. Ironically, some civil rights activists in Northern Ireland took to the streets to protest about these international problems more than about grievances closer to home. Unionists and nationalists would not remain insulated from the gathering storm of global protest for long.

Importantly, many IRA members saw their struggle in the context of worldwide national liberation struggles. Indeed, one former Provisional IRA volunteer admitted that at one time the organization had an 'embassy' in Algiers and had working contacts with the Popular Movement for the Liberation of Angola – Party of Labour (MPLA) and Zimbabwe African National Union – Patriotic Front (ZANU-PF). These links provided the IRA with much-needed logistical and financial support, as well as higher profile contacts with Colonel Gaddafi's Libyan regime and the African National Congress in South Africa. In an interview with the author the same IRA volunteer said:

[I]n reality I mean the contexts were good… Giving
people solidarity who were fighting a post-colonial
conflict… To me it consolidated my belief that we were
an internationalist group. That they could relate to our
struggle because we were socialist and secular, you know.
It wasn't just a nationalist push which inevitably, fatally,
alas it turned out to be.

Loyalists tended to look closer to home, by seeking
support for their cause in Glasgow and Merseyside. One
historian, Ian S. Wood, has charted how this support has
manifested itself in what he calls '90-minute Loyalists',
a term used to denote Northern Ireland soccer fans who
regularly attend Glasgow Rangers football matches. In
London, the UDA had a long-established brigade, which
was tasked with fundraising for the organization's front-
line units back in Northern Ireland. The London brigade
was largely inactive in the 1970s and 1980s until it was
taken over by Kentish Town militant Frank Portinari.
Portinari had joined the UDA in the mid-1980s and
rose to prominence soon afterwards. He was arrested,
along with two other men, in May 1993 while in
possession of weapons intended for the UDA in Belfast.
Throughout his time as UDA leader in Great Britain
Portinari rejuvenated the group's support base on the
UK mainland, placing him in a key role as the group
embraced the peace process after his release from prison.

Exporting the struggle

The threat posed by Irish republican terrorists was a long-
standing one and dated back to Irish Republican bomb
attacks in London in the late 19th century. In December
1867, in an attempt to free one of their incarcerated
members, the secretive Fenian Brotherhood carried out a
bomb attack on Clerkenwell Prison, London. The lavish
use of dynamite meant that the Fenians demolished a
row of houses nearby, killing 12 people and injuring over
50. As the celebrated Communist thinker Karl Marx
observed at the time:

The London masses, who have shown great sympathy towards Ireland, will be made wild and driven into the arms of a reactionary government. One cannot expect the London proletarians to allow themselves to be blown up in honour of Fenian emissaries.

Nevertheless, bombs in England became the powerful signature piece of each new incarnation of militant Irish republicanism over the next century. The threat of bombing would remain a thorn in the side of successive British governments, who were more susceptible to public calls for a solution to the 'Irish problem' to be found. IRA supporters in Catholic parts of mainland Britain helped the IRA export its armed struggle to England in the 1970s, 1980s and 1990s.

As a means of putting further pressure on the British state, the IRA took its war abroad, to military garrisons in Germany, the Netherlands and Gibraltar. In 1987 the

Three Provisional IRA members, Dan McCann, Mairead Farrell and Sean Savage, were shot dead by the SAS on 6 March 1988. The trio planned to explode a huge car bomb. (Daily Mail/Shutterstock)

IRA shot and killed an RAF serviceman in Roermond, near the German-Dutch border. Half an hour later the IRA blew up a car outside a nightclub in the village of Nieuwbergen, killing two RAF servicemen. In a statement released to the BBC, the IRA said '[w]e have a simple statement for Mrs Thatcher: Disengage from Ireland and there will be peace. If not, there will be no haven for your military personnel, and you will regularly be at airports awaiting your dead.' The IRA had now opened up a new front in its campaign of terror.

In perhaps one of the most controversial episodes in the Troubles, three IRA volunteers were killed by the SAS in Gibraltar on 6 March 1988. Although they had been unarmed at the time they were shot, intelligence suggested that the IRA suspects were preparing a car bomb aimed at British military personnel taking part in a parade. It had striking similarities with the Hyde Park outrage a number of years earlier. The 'Gibraltar Three', as they were later known, became martyrs for the republican cause, and their deaths led to an outpouring of sympathy for the IRA not only from within the nationalist community in Northern Ireland, but in Irish diaspora communities abroad.

The search for peace

Nationalists and republicans have always found sympathy and support in the many Irish diaspora communities scattered around the world, from the United States to Australia. The US connection, in particular, has borne both lucrative financial and moral support, as well as a steady flow of weapons. Throughout the Troubles, the British government was at pains to exert political pressure on those in the US who were offering their sympathies and support to violent republicanism. In a speech to Irish American corporate businessmen in 1977, Roy Mason challenged his audience to reconsider their support for militant republicanism. 'It is through machinery, not machine guns; through business not bombs that the people of this great nation can assist the tiny but very

Sinn Féin President Gerry Adams pictured with Irish Taoiseach Albert Reynolds and SDLP leader John Hume on 6 September 1994. Adams and Hume had been in political talks in 1993. (Photo by Mathieu Polak/ Sygma/ Sygma via Getty Images)

deserving area of Northern Ireland to continue along the road to normality and prosperity,' he said.

That the IRA could command support from Irish diaspora communities abroad allowed those who were arguing for an end to hostilities in the early 1990s to situate their 'armed struggle' within the broader international environment. Such thinking was advanced by the IRA in its so-called Tactical Use of Armed Struggle (TUAS) document in the 1990s. Placing the IRA's armed struggle in a broader context allowed Gerry Adams and those dedicated to the Sinn Féin 'peace strategy' to forge ahead on the political front.

The transition from war to peace in the wake of the 1994 paramilitary ceasefires was by no means a smooth one. Under John Major the British government was insistent on decommissioning prior to entering any form of talks about the future of Northern Ireland. They had appointed US Senator George Mitchell as chairman of the international body on arms decommissioning, which was an integral component of the British and Irish governments' 'twin-track' process to address this outstanding issue. Mitchell was later asked to stay on to chair the all-party talks that had evolved out of the bilateral negotiations between the political parties and both governments. Although the IRA was not formally part of the negotiations that led up to the Belfast Agreement of 10 April 1998, it was represented by Sinn Féin.

Addressing members of the Provisional IRA in 2005, Adams said that he had always 'defended the right of the IRA to engage in armed struggle', doing so on the basis that 'there was no alternative for those who would not bend the knee, or turn a blind eye to oppression, or for those who wanted a national republic'. However, with the onset of the peace process, he emphasized to them that there was now an 'alternative'. In his mind, the alternative was 'by building political support for republican and democratic objectives across Ireland and by winning support for these goals internationally'. Adams successfully convinced the IRA of the need to create the conditions upon which a peace deal could be

President Bill Clinton's administration was seen as a third party mediator in the conflict in Northern Ireland. Here he is pictured in Derry/ Londonderry on December 1995. (Photo by Dirck Halstead/Getty Images)

made. Within days of his speech the organization had called a halt to its armed campaign, and by September 2005 had decommissioned the remainder of its weapons.

Throughout the early days of the Troubles the British government resisted any international interference in its handling of the security situation in Northern Ireland. It used its influence on the UN Security Council to block any attempts to internationalize the conflict. However, as the descent into chaos continued in the wake of the imposition of direct rule in 1972, this was no longer seen as sustainable. With the signing of the Sunningdale Agreement in 1973 and the Anglo-Irish Agreement in 1985 the British state warmed to the idea of greater intergovernmental co-operation with the Republic of Ireland, particularly in the realm of border security. Although unionists rejected the Anglo-Irish Agreement, they begrudgingly accepted a more prominent role for the Dublin government by the time of the Good Friday Agreement in 1998, once constitutional safeguards had been put in place and enshrined by international law.

Gerry Adams with former South African President Nelson Mandela on 2 October 2001. Mandela's colleague and ANC negotiator Cyril Ramaphosa served as an inspector for the International Commission on Decommissioning. (ALEXANDER JOE/AFP via Getty Images)

HOW THE WAR ENDED
Ceasefire to Agreement

The Northern Ireland Troubles could not be defined as a war according to the strict criteria laid down by international law, or, indeed, in the conventional military sense, of uniformed armies facing each other on a carefully defined battlefield where the 'normal' rules of warfare govern chivalrous acts of mortal combat. Nevertheless, for many military personnel who deployed on Operation *Banner* the Troubles were a 'long war' few thought would ever end. That the Troubles did eventually subside, however, is in itself intriguing and worthy of further examination.

The late 1980s saw an upsurge in violence in Northern Ireland. The shooting of the three IRA volunteers in Gibraltar was followed by an attack on their funerals by loyalist terrorist Michael Stone. His killing of an IRA member that day saw republicans attack a car carrying two soldiers who had mistakenly driven into the cortege. The soldiers, Corporals Derek Wood and David Howes, were abducted by the IRA, who took them away, stripped them naked and shot them in the head. One of the first on the scene was a local priest, Father Alec Reid.

Father Reid had been close to Sinn Féin President Gerry Adams and following an approach by Dr Eberhard Spiecker, a fellow clergyman from Duisburg in West Germany, Reid travelled with political representatives from the Ulster Unionist Party, Democratic Unionist Party, SDLP and cross-community Alliance Party to Dr Spiecker's hometown to discuss the basis for ending the armed conflict. News of the summit leaked to the press in early 1989 and its significance was denied by the main party leaders. Nevertheless, the ground had now been prepared for Father Reid to meet with British government officials at the behest of Gerry Adams.

Publicly, new ground was also broken in a series of meetings between Gerry Adams and John Hume in 1989 and again in 1992. The 'Hume-Adams dialogue', as it became known, was a process aimed at healing rifts in the nationalist community and finding a united way out of the armed conflict. For Hume it also served to focus attention on the need to build confidence between the Provisionals and the British state.

Although there was a break in the secret dialogue between republicans and the British state for much of the 1980s, one British intelligence officer reactivated his link with the group via an intermediary called Brendan Duddy, a businessman from Derry/Londonderry. Duddy facilitated a meeting between the intelligence officer and Martin McGuinness, which led to a more sustained engagement between both parties. Although the contact was formally denied by the British and Sinn Féin, news leaked out in October 1993, causing embarrassment. Nevertheless, it had achieved its objective of laying the groundwork for future political compromise.

In the meantime, loyalist paramilitaries had nominated Protestant community representatives as the conduits through which information was shared between Reid and the IRA in Belfast. Loyalists also

Gerry Adams pictured with Martin McGuinness on 31 August 1994, the day of the IRA ceasefire. The IRA returned to war in 1996, before returning to negotiations in 1997. (GERRY PENNY/ AFP via Getty Images)

reached out to the British and Irish governments, asking the Revd Robin Eames, Anglican Archbishop of Armagh, to communicate directly with London, while the Irish-based trades union activist Chris Hudson spoke to Dublin.

All these individual streams trickled into the fast-flowing tide that eventually contributed to ceasefires being called, first by the IRA, and then by loyalists. The IRA's statement read

> Recognising the potential of the current situation and in order to enhance the democratic process and underlying our definitive commitment to its success, the leadership of the IRA have decided that as of midnight, August 31, there will be a complete cessation of military operations. All our units have been instructed accordingly.

With the republican ceasefire in place, the onus was now on loyalist paramilitary groupings to respond. The leaderships of the UVF and the UDA held secret meetings to thrash out the details of their own cessation of hostilities. As the UVF's Chief of Staff revealed in an interview with the author:

> Every UVF unit was consulted. There was no real opposition in the ranks – some worries and some scepticism but no outright opposition. Many of the politically motivated UVF members did have worries [but] the message was clear, the UVF is a counter-terrorist outfit. If PIRA [Provisional IRA] aggression stops then the UVF has no military role to play. The next stage would be a political one. The message to the UVF troops on the ground was that if the PIRA stops, we stop because the Union is safe, next stage is for our political representatives – this message was also sent to the Nationalist community. When the PIRA called its ceasefire, it proved that the analysis of the UVF leadership had been correct – this helped to lend it credibility.

Although the terms of reference for the ceasefire were agreed in secret in Monkstown on the outskirts of North Belfast, the wording of the statement was typed in the back office of the UVF-linked Progressive Unionist Party in its headquarters on the Shankill Road by 'Gusty' Spence, the veteran UVF commander. Spence later read out the ceasefire statement at a press conference called by the Combined Loyalist Military Command, an umbrella group bringing together the UVF/RHC and UDA/UFF. In it he expressed 'abject and true remorse' on behalf of loyalist paramilitaries, something which went further than the IRA's statement in recognizing the suffering inflicted on all innocent victims.

Scenes of jubilation followed in the wake of both ceasefires, albeit tinged with a sense of nervous optimism. Ceasefires had been tried before in the mid-1970s, but had not held. This time, however, there was a sense that conditions were different. By the early 1990s all paramilitary groups had a strong degree of cohesion, central control and discipline. As Malachi O'Doherty wrote in his insightful book on the IRA, *The Trouble with Guns*, '[a] ceasefire is a military operation. The authority of military leaders is required to maintain it.' O'Doherty maintained that although it was difficult to come to terms with people in the republican and loyalist groupings who may have murdered hundreds of people, 'when they have taken the job of containing their own murderous followers, through the authority they have acquired over those people by leading them to murder, then our interests in them are reversed'. Chillingly, the ceasefires and ensuing peace process, however imperfect, depended on paramilitary enforcers to take action that kept the violent conflict from re-emerging on the same scale as before.

The ceasefires did not completely silence the guns. It soon became obvious that dissent was growing within paramilitary ranks about the moves toward peace. On the one hand there had been disquiet in republican circles about John Major's insistence on IRA decommissioning before Sinn Féin could be admitted into peace talks. On the other hand, unionist trepidations about the inclusion of Sinn Féin in inter-party talks boiled over into outright hostility. Here the unionists held a trump card in that their representation at Westminster became an important bargaining chip with Major's minority Conservative government. Both the UUP leader James Molyneaux and his counterpart in the DUP Ian Paisley were diametrically opposed to talks between the British government and Sinn Féin. In Parliamentary debates on the Downing Street Declaration, Major said that 'there must be the clearest possible public renunciation of violence and then a decontamination period' before Sinn Féin could be admitted into talks. This provoked a crisis within republicanism, with hard-line elements vowing to restart the armed campaign.

One particular part of the IRA based in South Armagh had always held considerable sway within the wider movement and its continuing support of the IRA's Army Council's decision to call a ceasefire and enter talks with the British would be crucial. When it faltered, as it did in February 1996, its objections precipitated the IRA's return to war. During this period the IRA took its war to Britain, detonating a series of bombs across London and also huge car bombs in London's Docklands and Manchester city centre, causing millions of pounds worth of damage. One double car bomb attack on HQNI on 7 October 1996 claimed the life of a British soldier, Sergeant Major James Bradwell, and wounded 31 others. It appeared that the IRA had returned to its war of attrition.

However, the political context soon shifted when the British Labour Party under the leadership of Tony Blair was elected in the May 1997 general election. The Labour Party had advocated a policy of a united Ireland by consent since the 1970s. Under Blair it moved to sideline its powerful 'Brits out' pressure groups, such as the Troops Out Movement. New Labour's inclusive approach to the peace process helped to create the conditions under which the IRA renewed its ceasefire in July 1997. Within a short space of time Sinn Féin had

British Prime Minister Tony Blair with Irish Taoiseach Bertie Ahern and the US talks chairman Senator George Mitchell at the signing of the Good Friday Agreement on 10 April 1998. (DAN CHUNG/AFP via Getty Images)

been re-admitted into all-party talks, which eventually led to the signing of the Belfast/Good Friday Agreement on 10 April 1998.

Apart from reassuring unionists that their position within the union was safe until a majority of people in the province voted otherwise, New Labour's approach to the security situation emphasized a policy of 'normalization'. Normalization essentially meant the return of the British Army to barracks, soldiers exchanging helmets for berets, and the removal of Security Forces bases and watchtowers from Northern Ireland's landscape.

Between 1999 and 2004, the Army withdrew from eight bases it shared with the police. The figure was further reduced in the four years leading up to the end of Operation *Banner* on 31 July 2007. Similarly, between 1999 and 2004, ten observation and communications posts were closed and by July 2005 the number had been further reduced.

Nevertheless, the hastening of the normalization process was made more difficult by clashes between unionists and nationalists at Orange Order parades in places like Drumcree, near Portadown, and on the Springfield Road in West Belfast. Despite civil disturbances for much of the early to mid-2000s, the paramilitary groups moved to end their armed campaigns indefinitely. In July 2005 the IRA finally announced an end to its armed campaign:

> The leadership of Óglaigh na hÉireann 'has formally ordered an end to the armed campaign. This will take effect from 4pm this afternoon.
> All IRA units have been ordered to dump arms.
> All Volunteers have been instructed to assist the development of purely political and democratic programmes through exclusively peaceful means. Volunteers must not engage in any other activities whatsoever.

This announcement was made against growing instability on the streets of Belfast. In September 2005 the Army was deployed in support of the police in one

The last major public order deployment for the British Army was on the west Belfast 'peace-line' in September 2005, 36 years after its first major deployment in the same area. (Crispin Rodwell)

A Parachute Regiment soldier dismantles the observation post Golf One Zero at Creevekeeran near Crossmaglen in South Armagh. The Army reduced its military footprint in line with Provisional IRA decommissioning. (Paul McErlane / Alamy Stock Photo)

of the most ironic twists of the Troubles. British soldiers found themselves back on the streets of West Belfast to contain violence perpetrated mainly by loyalists on the Shankill Road, the site of the Army's first major public order operation in October 1969.

Following a period of further negotiations between the British and Irish governments and the two main political parties, the DUP and Sinn Féin, Ian Paisley sat down to a agree a power-sharing deal with his arch-nemesis Gerry Adams in May 2007. Later that summer the UVF announced it had 'put its arms beyond use' and in 2009 it joined the UDA in disarming. While the winding-down of the military dimension effectively removed the threat of the gun from Northern Irish politics, it did not bring an end to sectarianism or the underlying causes of the Troubles.

CONCLUSION AND CONSEQUENCES
The harsh lessons of the Troubles

Operation *Banner* ended on 31 July 2007. In its final 24 months all military surveillance posts were dismantled, the number of military installations fell from 24 sites to 13, and the total number of military helicopter flying hours also dropped dramatically. Importantly, all troops had been withdrawn to barracks and the number stationed in Northern Ireland fell to peace-time levels. Having become a byword for civil unrest, sectarian assassination and soldiers on the streets, Northern Ireland entered an uncertain future.

Armed conflicts of this kind are typically followed by an audit of their causes and consequences. Those directly affected by the violence may be in search of reasons why it happened and keen to address the awful legacy of violence. Often, the parties to an ethnic conflict – such as the groups and communities diametrically opposed to each other – look back at what happened through rose-tinted glasses. It is unsurprising, therefore, that debates over the past in Northern Ireland have become more audible since the sound of gunfire and explosions has faded into the background.

Drawing lessons from armed conflicts is fraught with many pitfalls. Not all of them have similar causes, continuities and consequences. While it is tempting to draw comparisons between the British Army's involvement in Northern Ireland and how it has approached contemporary operations elsewhere, such as in Iraq and Afghanistan, one must be careful not to make too many bold assumptions. Reflecting on his involvement in bringing an end to the Troubles, former prime minister Tony Blair said, 'I know this from the Middle East peace process now, that I'm engaged in intimately, that one of the things that gives them hope is the success of the Northern Ireland process. It's a big symbol of change and possibility right round the world.' While this might have been true then, we know from hindsight that it never amounted to anything. Thanks to Tony Blair and other Western leaders like him who pursued an interventionist agenda, the Middle East became more unstable. The flaw in the approach was when they adopted it as a model or template for ending other armed conflicts, rather than merely an inspiration for conflict resolution.

Military lessons learned

Reflecting back over his 50-year career as a soldier, Field Marshal Bernard Montgomery concluded in his memoirs that '[w]e cannot see into the future accurately. But we can at least ensure that we do not disregard the lessons of the past: only a madman would do that.' As an institution the British Army actively sought to capture its own lessons from its deployment in Northern Ireland. These ranged from attempts to disseminate tactical lessons through doctrine notes and training serials to the execution of major and minor operations in a similar way to those executed during the Troubles and peace process. In one Army doctrine note entitled *Operation Banner: An Analysis of Military Operations in Northern Ireland*, the authors suggested that the campaign was – on balance – a success, but they highlighted several key points for consideration when approaching future operations elsewhere.

The first was that there had never been an overall campaign authority for Operation *Banner*. Here the pamphlet argued that the decision-making process was chaotic at times and resulted in – among other things – the intelligence agencies working to different agendas. Nevertheless, it is no coincidence that the Provisional IRA reorganized for its 'long war' strategy in the late 1970s, adopting a cellular unit structure, just as Britain's covert operations gathered some forward momentum. As we would discover with the publication of the Iraq Inquiry chaired by former Northern Ireland Permanent Under Secretary Sir John Chilcot, British military operations in Iraq between 2003 and 2009 also lacked an overarching campaign authority and lack of a coherent strategy. It is difficult to see how it could have been otherwise, when the Army played a supporting role for the civil authorities in Northern Ireland and to the United States in Iraq.

Many of the Land Rover vehicles used on the streets of Northern Ireland were repainted desert colour and sent to Basra. They became known as 'cooking pots' by soldiers. (Edwards Collection)

At a tactical level the Army learned a huge amount from Operation *Banner*. The Army's training regime was second to none in preparing troops for deployment in-theatre, taking soldiers through tutorials on the IRA's arsenal of weapons and its bomb-making techniques, as well as its use of shoot-and-scoot tactics and armed propaganda (the use of violence to influence the wider political context). All this corporate knowledge came at a price, however, as it was built up from the direct exposure to terrorist violence. In terms of patrolling on foot and in soft-skinned vehicles, Explosive Ordnance Disposal work and in public order drills, the Army would take this forward in its intervention in Iraq in 2003–2009.

Perhaps the biggest single stimulant in the Army's lesson-learning process was the decision by senior military commanders to take steps to avoid repeating mistakes. This willingness to admit its mistakes – while actively taking steps to ensure they are not repeated – is a prime example of the Army's professional ability to learn and adapt in highly pressurized environments. Reflecting on the release of the Saville Inquiry* report into 'Bloody Sunday', the Chief of the General Staff (subsequently Chief of the Defence Staff) Sir David Richards said:

> We must never forget the tragic events of Bloody Sunday. In the 38 years since that tragic day's events, lessons have been learned. The way the Army is trained, the way it works and the way it operates have all changed significantly.

Joining General Richards in his comments, his predecessor General Sir Mike Jackson, himself a veteran of several deployments on Operation *Banner*, said:

---

*   Lord Saville was chosen by the New Labour government to head up the 'Bloody Sunday' Inquiry in 1998. A former High Court Judge, he was appointed a Law Lord in 1997 and went on to become Justice of the Supreme Court of the United Kingdom between 2009 and 2010. He was hand-picked because he was considered to be 'less stuffy' and more of 'a modernizing judge', who could navigate a route through the choppy waters of this emotionally intense episode in Northern Ireland's past.

I recall that nearly 40 years ago in Northern Ireland the situation was grim with significant loss of life on all sides – not least by the Army. Over the 38 years of the Army's operational deployment in the province the vast majority of the some 250,000 soldiers who served there behaved admirably, often in the face of severe provocation, and with the loss of several hundred lives and 6,000 wounded. Northern Ireland today is now a very different place, not least because of those sacrifices and I ask that Lord Saville's report be seen in this context.

The Army had indeed learnt valuable lessons in Northern Ireland, just as it has done in all of its operational theatres since 1945.

Notwithstanding these candid admissions, there has also been a tendency to learn the wrong lessons from Operation *Banner*. The Army's doctrine note, for instance, said that the 'few bombs that were placed in Service married quarters areas appear to have been placed to tie down troops, rather than to kill or maim. The reasons probably lie in the self-image of the IRA as an Army with its own sense of morality, honour and justice.' While on the face of it such monochrome remembrances of the Troubles are harmless, they serve to seriously underplay the ruthlessness of terrorist groups like the IRA. Moreover, by playing up the political 'nobility' of the republican campaign this account obscures the brutal reality of IRA violence and constructs misleading interpretations out of bad history.

Rather than consciously avoid casualties among its opponents, the IRA deliberately targeted Security Forces personnel and the civilians working for them. In 1972 the Official IRA carried out a no-warning bombing of 2 Para's mess in Aldershot Army Garrison, Hampshire, killing six civilian workers and a Roman Catholic padre. In the late 1980s the IRA attempted to mortar the families' quarters at the UDR's Steeple barracks in Antrim. And in perhaps the most brazen attempt to kill and maim Security Forces personnel, the IRA detonated two huge car bombs in Thiepval Barracks in October 1996. In undertaking these operations and countless others, the IRA rightly earned its reputation as one of the most ruthless terrorist organizations in history.

Political lessons learned

Like the Army, the British government also learned lessons from its long involvement in Northern Ireland. In a speech to the Mid-Atlantic Club in Washington, DC, on 17 October 1977 the Northern Ireland Secretary of State, Roy Mason, said: 'Perhaps one of the most important lessons learned in Northern Ireland over the past few years – and it is a lesson which has important international implications – is that in a democratic society there is no way forward through the use of violence.'

This was a recurrent theme in the government's official language throughout the Troubles. It dovetailed with security policy in implying that there could be no military solution to the conflict. Thus, the main task of the police and Army was to stabilize the security situation while various political initiatives were attempted, from the Sunningdale Agreement in 1973 through to the Good Friday Agreement in 1998. The political context was vitally important as it permitted the British government to enter into negotiations with the Provisional IRA at opportune moments in the 1970s, 1980s and 1990s. In the words of veteran journalist Malachi O'Doherty:

> Another lesson for militants and state security forces: don't kill anybody unless you really have to. Especially, do not kill the leaders of the militant groups. If you want leaders to be able to control the whole movement underneath them, then you have to leave them in place for long enough to secure credibility and influence. Don't fragment an enemy you ultimately hope to negotiate with.

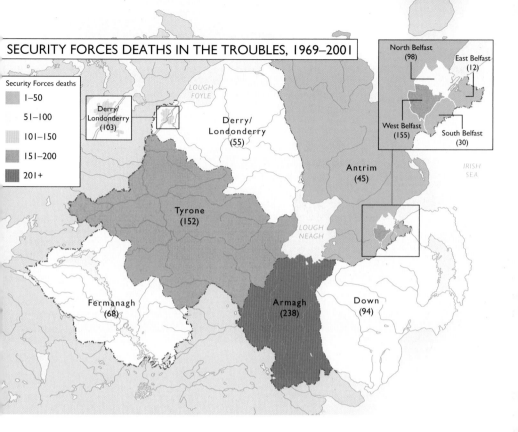

North Belfast
(98)

East Belfast
(12)

West Belfast
(155)

South Belfast
(30)

Security Forces deaths

1–50

51–100

101–150

151–200

201+

Derry/
Londonderry
(103)

Derry/
Londonderry
(55)

LOUGH
FOYLE

Antrim
(45)

IRISH
SEA

Tyrone
(152)

LOUGH
NEAGH

Fermanagh
(68)

Armagh
(238)

Down
(94)

The willingness of states to 'talk to terrorists' has become more evident since the bedding-down of the peace process in the late 1990s. The merits of dialogue between representatives of the various terrorist groups and the British and Irish governments have been recognized and applauded on the world stage. However, it is often forgotten how political space was created only in the wake of an application of coercion, mainly on the part of the British government and its Security Forces, both to cajole and entice these groups into suing for peace. From the late 1970s the British government returned to the first principle that in combating terrorism and insurgency, the lead must always be taken by the civilian authority. Only when the police and armed forces accepted the need to become more coordinated in a way that supported government policy was it assured that terrorism could be truly defeated in a strategic sense.

The human cost

Approximately 3,700 people were killed during the Northern Ireland Troubles. Although the number of deaths might seem small compared with the total population of the region, which sat around 1.5 million throughout the conflict, scaled proportionately, had the violence taken place in Great Britain, it would have claimed 100,000 lives, or 500,000 in the United States. Without question, the single biggest group affected during the Troubles was the local civilian population, with around half of those killed thought to be non-combatants. Further examination of these statistics reveals that around twice as many Catholic civilians were killed than Protestant civilians. However, the Protestant unionist community saw the deaths of locally recruited Security Forces in the RUC and UDR/Royal Irish Regiment Home Service as specifically targeting them. The bloodiest year of the Troubles was 1972, when 497 people died, the vast majority of whom were civilians.

Although the number of RUC officers killed in the line of duty has been reliably recorded as 301 by the

Queen Elizabeth II awarded the Conspicuous Gallantry Cross to the UDR and Home Service battalions of the Royal Irish Regiment in 2006. A total of 197 serving UDR soldiers were murdered in the Troubles. (Photo by PETER MUHLY/AFP via Getty Images)

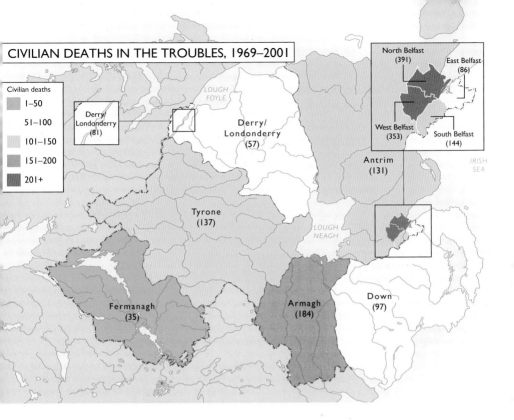

CIVILIAN DEATHS IN THE TROUBLES, 1969–2001

Civilian deaths
- 1–50
- 51–100
- 101–150
- 151–200
- 201+

LOUGH FOYLE

Derry/Londonderry (81)

Derry/Londonderry (57)

North Belfast (391)

East Belfast (86)

West Belfast (353)

South Belfast (144)

Antrim (131)

IRISH SEA

Tyrone (137)

LOUGH NEAGH

Fermanagh (35)

Armagh (184)

Down (97)

RUC George Cross Foundation and Police Service of Northern Ireland, the total number of British military personnel to have died is contested. As Operation *Banner* drew down in 2007 the then Chief of the Defence Staff, Sir Jock Stirrup, put the number of fatalities at 651 with 6,307 wounded, while an official MoD tally from 2008 recorded a total of 763 (and 6,116 wounded), a figure which includes 651 Army and Royal Marines personnel, one Royal Navy serviceman, 50 members of the UDR/Royal Irish Regiment, ten members of the Territorial Army, and 51 military personnel murdered outside Northern Ireland. The Ministry of Defence did not release an official record of the number of troops killed in Northern Ireland until 2020, when the government finally admitted that 1,441 members of the armed forces had died in Operation *Banner*. It recorded the number of those killed as a result of hostile action in Northern Ireland as 722, with 22 killed as a result of hostile action outside Northern Ireland.

A further 719 died of other causes while on duty. These statistics were only publicly released after the tireless campaigning of Operation *Banner* veteran and author Ken Wharton, who had compiled similar statistics in his numerous books.

However, these statistics mask the oft-forgotten truth that 40 former members of the UDR and 18 former members of the RUC died at the hands of republican terrorists, for the IRA did not distinguish between on-duty, off-duty and former members. Drilling down deeper into these statistics, we can also see that the most dangerous areas for Security Forces personnel throughout the Troubles were County Armagh, West Belfast and County Tyrone.

In comparable terms it could be argued that Operation *Banner* was more intense in terms of deaths and injuries in the line of duty than Operation *Telic*, the British intervention in Iraq, where 135 out of a total number of 178 British service personnel died as a direct result of hostile action between 2003 and 2009. Operation *Herrick*, the British armed forces' involvement in Afghanistan, saw 405 troops out of 457 killed in hostile action. The year 2009 was the bloodiest for British forces deployed in Afghanistan, with 108 military personnel killed in action. Nevertheless, Northern Ireland in 1972 remains the worst year for British military deaths in the post-war era, with some 130 troops killed in hostilities.

Despite the number of deaths and casualties of British service personnel, Operation *Banner* was the most successful deployment of the UK's armed forces in the late 20th century. It ended as it had begun, with troops deployed on the streets to keep an uneasy peace between two communities who found it impossible to reconcile their differences peacefully.

CHRONOLOGY

1920	Government of Ireland Act passed, partitioning Ireland into North and South
1922	Formation of the RUC
1939–1940	IRA bombing campaign in England
1941	**April–May** Belfast 'Blitz' by the German Luftwaffe
1956	**December** IRA launches its border campaign, Operation *Harvest*
1957	Internment temporarily introduced on both sides of the border
1962	**February** IRA calls a halt to Operation *Harvest* and dumps arms
1964	The Revd Ian Paisley leads protest march into Divis Street in the Falls Road area, sparking off three nights of intense rioting
1965	Ulster Volunteer Force (UVF) formed; former soldier 'Gusty' Spence appointed as its first commander
1966	50th anniversary of the Easter Rising heightens tensions; UVF murders several people across Belfast
1967	Northern Ireland Civil Rights Association (NICRA) formed
1968	**5 October** NICRA march turns violent in Duke Street, Derry/Londonderry
1969	**4 January** People's Democracy march from Belfast to Derry/Londonderry attacked by loyalists and Ulster Special Constabulary members ('B' Specials) at Burntollet
	28 April Northern Ireland's prime minister, Terence O'Neill, resigns from office
	10 August Rioting in Belfast and Derry/Londonderry
	14 August British troops deploy onto Northern Ireland's streets
	October British troops are involved in containing a massive riot by loyalists in the Shankill area of West Belfast

December IRA splits into Official and Provisional wings

1970 **April** 'B' Specials disbanded; Ulster Defence Regiment formed

3–5 July Falls Road Curfew

1971 **6 February** First British Army soldier, Gunner Robert Curtis, killed by the IRA

9 August Internment reintroduced

1972 **30 January** Soldiers from 1st Battalion, The Parachute Regiment, open fire on civil rights marchers; 27 people are wounded, 14 fatally. It later becomes known as 'Bloody Sunday'

21 July The IRA detonates 22 bombs across Belfast, killing nine people and injuring hundreds on 'Bloody Friday'

31 July Operation *Motorman* is launched to retake 'no-go' areas. The Provisional IRA explodes three bombs in Claudy, County Londonderry, killing nine people, including a child

1974 **4 February** The IRA kills 11 (including two young children) when it blows up a coach carrying off-duty soldiers and their families

May Loyalist strike brings down power-sharing experiment

5 October The IRA carries out the bombings of two Guildford pubs, killing four people

21 November The IRA bombs two Birmingham pubs, killing 19

1976 **5 January** IRA gunmen execute ten Protestant civilians in Kingsmill, South Armagh; another is wounded

November The IRA reorganizes along cellular lines

1977 Overt military lead in security policy is scaled back in favour of 'police primacy'

1979 **30 March** Airey Neave MP, former Colditz prison escapee and close confidant of Margaret Thatcher, is assassinated by the Irish National Liberation Army (INLA) when a bomb explodes under his car at the House of Commons

27 August Lord Mountbatten, the Queen's cousin and former Chief of the Defence Staff, is blown up

by the IRA; 18 British Army soldiers are killed by
the IRA in a bomb attack near Warrenpoint

1981   **5 May** Bobby Sands becomes the first IRA hunger
striker to die, after 66 days' fasting. Nine other IRA
and INLA prisoners follow suit

1982   **6 December** The INLA bombs the Droppin' Well
pub in Ballykelly, killing 17 people, including 11
off-duty soldiers based in the town

1983   'Supergrass' trials publicly identify leading terrorists

1984   Gerry Adams begins secret dialogue with the
British government

1985   **15 November** The Anglo-Irish Agreement is signed
between the British and Irish governments; start of
'Ulster Says No' campaign

1987   **8 May** Elite SAS soldiers kill eight IRA terrorists
in Loughgall
8 November The IRA detonates a no-warning
bomb next to the war memorial in Enniskillen,
killing 11 people and injuring 63

1988   **6 March** SAS team kills three IRA terrorists
in Gibraltar
16 March Michael Stone, of the Ulster Freedom
Fighters (UFF), attacks the funerals of the
'Gibraltar Three'
19 March Two off-duty soldiers are abducted and
shot dead by the IRA after mistakenly driving into a
republican funeral cortège
October Secret talks between the main political
parties are facilitated by German clergyman and
peace-builder Dr Eberhard Spiecker in Duisburg,
West Germany; the Provisional IRA and Sinn Féin
send Father Alec Reid to represent their interests

1990   **24 October** The IRA uses human bomb tactic,
killing several soldiers

1991   **7 February** The IRA mortars 10 Downing Street;
Prime Minister John Major and his cabinet are
holding a meeting to discuss the Gulf War.

1992   **1 July** The Ulster Defence Regiment is amalgamated
with The Royal Irish Rangers to form The Royal
Irish Regiment

10 August The Ulster Defence Association (UDA), the largest loyalist paramilitary group, is banned by the British government

1993   **23 October** Shankill Road bombing by the IRA kills nine civilians

1994   **9, 11 & 13 March** The IRA mortars Heathrow Airport
31 August The IRA ends its military hostilities
13 October Loyalist paramilitaries announce a ceasefire

1995   Talks between British and Irish government and paramilitary representatives

1996   **9 February** The IRA detonates a massive bomb in Canary Wharf, London, heralding an end to its ceasefire
30 May Forum Election
15 June The IRA bombs Manchester city centre
July Orange Order parade at Drumcree, County Armagh, leads to widespread civil disturbances in Northern Ireland
7 October The IRA attacks British Army HQ in Lisburn, with two 500lb (227kg) bombs, killing one soldier and injuring 20 other people

1997   **12 February** Lance Bombardier Stephen Restorick is killed by a sniper; he is the last soldier to die in Operation *Banner*
20 July The IRA reinstates its ceasefire

1998   **10 April** The Belfast/Good Friday Agreement is signed
15 August The Real IRA, an ultra-republican splinter group, explodes a no-warning car bomb in Omagh, County Tyrone, killing 29 people and two unborn children

1999   **29 November** Power-sharing executive appointed
2 December Direct rule ends; power devolved to Stormont

2000   Loyalist feud between the UDA/UFF and the UVF/RHC (Red Hand Commando, a small paramilitary group with close ties to the UVF)

2001   The 'Holy Cross dispute' in Ardoyne, North Belfast, sees British troops once again deployed in a major operation to keep the peace

2002	An IRA spy ring is uncovered at Stormont, prompting the collapse of the power-sharing executive and suspension of devolution
2005	**28 July** The IRA calls an end to its armed campaign **September** Annual Whiterock Orange Order parade in West Belfast ends in the worst rioting in three decades, prompting the deployment of British soldiers in support of the PSNI; the IRA decommissions the last of its weapons and explosives
2006	**October** Multi-party talks lead to the St Andrews Agreement
2007	**8 May** Devolution returns to Northern Ireland, as Ian Paisley and Gerry Adams agree to enter a power-sharing executive **31 July** Operation *Banner* ends

FURTHER READING

Primary sources
Archives

The National Archives of the United Kingdom (Kew, London):

CAB/129/144, 'Press notice following meeting between Home Secretary James Callaghan and influential Roman Catholic deputation from Belfast', dated 12 September 1969

CAB/128/48, 'Top Secret Meeting of the Cabinet', dated 27 July 1972

CJ 3/13, 'Relations with the Government of Northern Ireland: Formal Requests for Military Assistance and Subsequent Role of the Military', all documents dated August 1969

DEFE 70/214, Appended Letter to the document 'The Future of Internment', dated 14 February 1972

DEFE 70/644, 'IRA Mine Warfare – Command Detonated Mines', dated 7 August 1972

DEFE 24/1945, 'Armed Helicopters in Northern Ireland', dated 20 March 1973

DEFE 24/1226, 'Northern Ireland: Notes of Meetings', all documents dated 1976 and 1977

DEFE 24/1618, 'Working Group on Security Forces Capability', all documents dated 1977

DEFE 11/918, 'Possible Loyalist Disturbances in Northern Ireland', memos dated 26 and 27 April and 2 and 4 May 1977

DEFE 11/918, 'PM's Private Secretary to Northern Ireland Office', dated 28 April 1977

DEFE 11/918, 'Correspondence from Roy Mason to Fred Malley', dated 18 May 1977

DEFE 11/918, 'Directive for the General Officer Commanding Northern Ireland as Director of Military Operations', dated 28 July 1977

DEFE 11/918, 'Transcript of a Speech by Roy Mason to the Mid-Atlantic Club, Washington D.C.', dated 17 October 1977

DEFE 11/918, 'Commander Land Forces Operational Summary for the 2 Weeks ending 19 October 1977', dated 19 October 1977

FCO 87/221, 'Report by Frank Steele of a Visit to the Bogside and Creggan on 4 and 5 April 1973', dated 5 April 1973

PREM 15/1009, 'Top Secret: Notes of a Meeting with Representatives of the Provisional IRA', dated 21 June 1972

PREM 15/1011, 'Top Secret – Perimeter – Northern Ireland: Draft Rules of Engagement', dated 26 July 1972

Unknown reference, 'Report entitled 'Subversion in the UDR' prepared by British Military Intelligence in August 1973', dated August 1973. Available at: http://cain.ulst. ac.uk/publicrecords/1973/subversion_in_the_udr.htm (accessed 17 September 2010)

London School of Economics and Political Science Archives:
Papers of Merlyn Rees (Baron Merlyn-Rees), 1920–2006

Public Records Office of Northern Ireland (Belfast):
GOV 3/17/3, Correspondence between Lieutenant-General Sir Harry Tuzo and the Governor of Northern Ireland, Lord Grey of Naunton, relating to the security situation in border areas, dated 4 and 7 September 1971

PRONI, PM 5/2/1, Private letter from Dr Norman Laird, Stormont MP for St Anne's, to Major James Chichester-Clark, 27 September 1969

Special Collections, Bodleian Library:
Clement Attlee, Harold Wilson and James Callaghan Papers

Interviews

Interview with the leader of the UVF, 9 September 2004. This individual has allegedly commanded the organization since the 1970s

Interview with Billy Mitchell, 16 September 2005. Former high-ranking member of the UVF in the 1970s and Progressive Unionist Party strategist from the early 1990s until his death in 2006

Interview with a former British Army staff officer, 21 June 2010. A former major who manned the Army's 'press desk' at HQNI, 1970–73

Interview with Tommy Gorman, 23 June 2010. Former member of the Provisional IRA and senior operations officer in the Belfast Brigade's engineering department

Interview with Jon McCourt, 23 June 2010. Former member of the Derry IRA, 1969–75; now well-respected peace advocate in Derry City

Interview with a former member of 2 Para, and later the UDR/RIR, 31 August 2010. Served several tours throughout Northern Ireland in the 1970s, 1980s and 1990s

Interview with a former member of the UDR, 1 September 2010. Based in the County Derry/Londonderry area and who served from 1971 until 1992 in both a part-time and full-time capacity

Interview with a former Royal Engineers Search Adviser, 17 September 2010. Served several tours in the 1970s and 1980s

Interview with a former officer from the UDR/RIR, 22 September 2010. Based mainly in the County Antrim area

Official publications

Cameron, *Disturbances in Northern Ireland*, Presented to Parliament September 1969, Cmd. 532 (Belfast, 1969)

Independent Monitoring Commission, *Reports of the IMC, 2004–2010*. Accessed at: https://www.gov.uk/government/organisations/independent-monitoring-commission (accessed 21 September 2022)

Ministry of Defence, UK Armed Forces Deaths: Operational Deaths Post World War II, 3 September 1945 to 15 March 2020, London, 26 March 2020

Northern Ireland Community Relations Commission Research Unit, *Flight: A Report on Population Movement in Belfast during August 1971* (Belfast, 1971)

Northern Ireland House of Commons, *Parliamentary Debates: Official Report* (Hansard), 1921–72

Northern Ireland Office, *The Agreement, 1998*. Archived at: <https://www.gov.uk/government/publications/the-belfast-agreement> (accessed 21 September 2022)

Saville, *Report of the Bloody Sunday Inquiry*. Archived at: <https://www.gov.uk/government/publications/report-of-the-bloody-sunday-inquiry> (accessed 21 September 2022)

Scarman, *Violence and Civil Disturbances in Northern Ireland in 1969*. Presented to Parliament April 1972, Cmd. 566 (Belfast, 1972)

UK Parliament, Investigation of former Armed Forces personnel who served in Northern Ireland. Archived at: <https://commonslibrary.parliament.uk/research-briefings/cbp-8352/> (accessed 21 September 2022)

Secondary sources
Articles and book chapters

Benest, David, 'Aden to Northern Ireland, 1966–76' in Strachan, Hew, (ed.), *Big Wars and Small Wars: The British Army and the Lessons of War in the Twentieth Century*, London, 2006, pp. 115–44

Bennett, Huw, 'From Direct Rule to Motorman: Adjusting British Military Strategy for Northern Ireland in 1972', *Studies in Conflict and Terrorism*, 33(6) (June 2010), pp. 511–32

Dixon, Paul, 'Hearts and Minds? British Counter-insurgency in Northern Ireland', *Journal of Strategic Studies*, 32(3) (June 2009), pp. 445–74

Edwards, Aaron, 'Abandoning Armed Struggle? The Ulster Volunteer Force as a Case-study of Strategic Terrorism in Northern Ireland', *Studies in Conflict and Terrorism*, 32(2) (February 2009), pp. 146–66

Edwards, Aaron, 'Misapplying Lessons Learned? Analysing the Utility of British Counter-insurgency Strategy in Northern Ireland, 1971–76', *Small Wars and Insurgencies*, 21(2) (June 2010), pp. 303–30

Edwards, Aaron 'Deterrence, Coercion and Brute Force in Asymmetric Conflict: The Role of the Military Instrument in Resolving the Northern Ireland "Troubles"', *Dynamics of Asymmetric Conflict*, Special Edition on Conflict and Post-conflict in Northern Ireland, 4(3), (December 2011), pp. 226–41

Edwards, Aaron '"A whipping boy if ever there was one"? The British Army and the Politics of Civil-Military Relations in Northern Ireland, 1969–79', *Contemporary British History*, 28(2), (June 2014), pp. 166–89

Edwards, Aaron 'Practice without Principles? Northern Ireland and the Struggle against the Provisional IRA, 1969–2007' in Fremont-Barnes, G. (ed.) *A History of Counter-insurgency: Volume 2 – From Cyprus to Afghanistan, 1955 to the 21st Century*, Santa Barbara, 2015, pp. 255–76

Edwards, Aaron 'The Security Forces and Truth Recovery in Northern Ireland' in Dawson, G., S. Hopkins and J. Dover (eds) *The Northern Ireland Troubles in Britain: Impacts, Engagements, Legacies and Memories*, Manchester, 2016, pp. 300–315

Edwards, Aaron 'British Security Policy and the Sunningdale Agreement: The Consequences of Using Force to Combat Terrorism in a Liberal Democracy' in McCann, D. and C. McGrattan (eds) *Sunningdale, the Ulster Workers' Council Strike and the Struggle for Democracy in Northern Ireland*, Manchester, 2017, pp. 87–99

Edwards, Aaron 'Beating the Retreat on a Contested Past? The British Army and the Politics of Commemoration in Northern Ireland' in Smyth, J. (ed.), *Remembering the Troubles: Contesting the Recent Past in Northern Ireland*, Notre Dame, 2017, pp. 77–95

Edwards, Aaron '"Acting with Restraint and Courtesy, Despite Provocation?" Army Operations in Belfast During the Northern Ireland "Troubles", 1969–2007' in Fremont-Barnes, G. (ed.) *A History of Modern Urban Operations*, Basingstoke, 2020, pp. 287–319

Edwards, Aaron 'The Provisional IRA and the Elusive Concept of Winning' in Strohn, Matthias (ed.) *Winning Wars: The Enduring Nature and Changing Character of Victory from Antiquity to the 21st Century*, London, 2021, pp. 229–42

Grayson, Richard S., 'The Place of the First World War in Contemporary Irish Republicanism in Northern Ireland', *Irish Political Studies*, 25(3) (September 2010), pp. 325–45

Iron, Colonel Richard, 'Britain's Longest War: Northern Ireland, 1967–2007' in Marston, Daniel and Malkasian, Carter, (eds), *Counterinsurgency in Modern Warfare*, Oxford, 2009, pp. 167–84

Irwin, Sir Alistair, and Mahoney, Mike, 'The Military Response' in Dingley, James, (ed.), *Combating Terrorism in Northern Ireland*, London, 2009, pp. 198–226

Kirk-Smith, Michael, and Dingley, James, 'Countering Terrorism in Northern Ireland: The Role of Intelligence', *Small Wars and Insurgencies*, 20(3–4) (September–December 2009), pp. 551–73

McCleery, Martin J. and Aaron Edwards 'The 1988 Murders of Corporal David Howes and Corporal Derek Wood: A Micro-Dynamic Analysis of Political Violence during the Northern Ireland Conflict', *Critical Military Studies*, 5(2), (2019), pp. 131–49

Neumann, Peter R., 'Winning the "War on Terror"? Roy Mason's Contribution to Counter-terrorism in Northern Ireland', *Small Wars and Insurgencies*, 14(3) (Autumn 2003), pp. 45–64

Newsinger, John, 'From Counter-insurgency to Internal Security: Northern Ireland, 1969–1992', *Small Wars and Insurgencies*, 6(1) (Spring 1995), pp. 88–111

O'Dochartaigh, Niall, 'Bloody Sunday: Error or Design?', *Contemporary British History*, 24(1) (March 2010), pp. 89–108

O'Doherty, Malachi, 'Lessons from Northern Ireland', *The Guardian*, 8 May 2007

O'Doherty, Malachi, 'Blair's Flaky Credentials', *The Guardian*, 26 June 2007

O'Kane, Eamonn 'When Can Conflicts be Resolved? A Critique of Ripeness', *Civil Wars*, 8(3-4), (2006), pp. 268–84

O'Kane, Eamonn 'Learning from Northern Ireland? the Uses and Abuses of the Irish "Model"', *British Journal of Politics & International Relations*, 12(2), (2010), pp. 239–56

Books

Barthorp, Michael, *Crater to the Creggan: The History of the Royal Anglian Regiment, 1964–1974*, London, 1976

Bean, Kevin, *The New Politics of Sinn Féin*, Liverpool, 2007

Bew, John, Martyn Frampton, and Inigo Gurruchaga *Talking to Terrorists: Making Peace in Northern Ireland and the Basque Country*, London, 2009

Bew, Paul, *Ireland: The Politics of Enmity, 1789–2006*, Oxford, 2007

Bowyer Bell, J., *The IRA, 1968–2000: Analysis of a Secret Army*, London, 2000

Burke, Edward, *Army of Tribes: British Army Cohesion, Deviancy and Murder in Northern Ireland*, Liverpool, 2018

Callaghan, James, *A House Divided: The Dilemma of Northern Ireland*, London, 1973

Carlin, Willie, *Thatcher's Spy: My Life as an MI5 Agent inside Sinn Féin*, Newbridge, 2019

Clausewitz, Carl von, *On War*, edited and translated by Michael Howard and Peter Paret, Princeton, NJ, 1989

Collins, Eamon, *Killing Rage*, London, 1998

Dannatt, General Sir Richard, *Leading from the Front: The Autobiography*, London, 2010

Dewar, Lieutenant-Colonel Michael, *The British Army in Northern Ireland: Revised Edition*, London, 1985

Dillon, Martin, *The Dirty War*, London, 1991

Dillon, Martin, *The Shankill Butchers: A Case-study of Mass Murder*, London, 1991

Dillon, Martin, *Killer in Clowntown: Joe Doherty, the IRA and the Special Relationship*, London, 1992

Dillon, Martin, *Stone Cold: The True Story of Michael Stone and the Milltown Massacre*, London, 1993

Dixon, Paul, *Northern Ireland: The Politics of War and Peace: Second Edition*, Basingstoke, 2008

Edwards, Aaron, and Stephen Bloomer (eds), *Transforming the Peace Process in Northern Ireland: From Terrorism to Democratic Politics*, Dublin, 2008

Edwards, Aaron, *Defending the Realm? The Politics of Britain's Small Wars since 1945*, Manchester, 2012

Edwards, Aaron, *UVF: Behind the Mask*, Newbridge, 2017

Edwards, Aaron, *Agents of Influence: Britain's Secret Intelligence War Against the IRA*, Newbridge, 2021

English, Richard, *Armed Struggle: The History of the IRA*, London, 2003

Evelegh, Robin, *Peacekeeping in a Democratic Society*, London, 1978

Fulton, Kevin, *Double Agent: My Secret Life Undercover in the IRA*, London, 2019

Geraghty, Tony, *The Irish War: The Military History of a Domestic Conflict*, London, 1998

Hamill, Desmond, *Pig in the Middle: The Army in Northern Ireland, 1969–1984*, London, 1985

Hanley, Brian, and Scott Millar, *The Lost Revolution: The Story of the Official IRA and the Worker's Party*, Dublin, 2009

Harnden, Toby, *'Bandit Country': The IRA and South Armagh*, London, 2000

Hennessey, Thomas, *A History of Northern Ireland: 1921–1996*, Dublin, 1997

Hennessey, Thomas, *The Northern Ireland Peace Process: Ending the Troubles?*, Dublin, 2000

Hennessey, Thomas, *The Origins of the Troubles*, Dublin, 2005

Hennessey, Thomas, *The Evolution of the Troubles, 1970–72*, Dublin, 2007

Holland, Jack and Susan Phoenix, *Phoenix: Policing the Shadows – The Secret War against Terrorism in Northern Ireland*, London, 1996

Jackson, General Sir Mike, *Soldier: The Autobiography*, London, 2007

Kitson, Frank, *Low Intensity Operations: Subversion, Insurgency, Peacekeeping*, London, 1971

Kitson, Frank, *Bunch of Five*, London, 1977

Leahy, Thomas, *The Intelligence War Against the IRA*, Cambridge, 2020

McCleery, Martin J., *Operation Demetrius and its Aftermath: A New History of the Use of Internment without Trial in Northern Ireland 1971–75*, Manchester, 2015

McDonald, Henry, and John Cusack, *UVF: The Endgame*, Dublin, 2008

McGrattan, Cillian, *Northern Ireland, 1968–2008: The Politics of Retrenchment*, Basingstoke, 2010

McKittrick, David, Seamus Kelters, Brian Feeney, and Chris Thorton, *Lost Lives: The Stories of the Men, Women and Children who Died as a Result of the Northern Ireland Troubles*, Edinburgh, 2001

Matchett, William, *Secret Victory: The Intelligence War that Beat the IRA*, Lisburn, 2016

Moloney, Ed, *A Secret History of the IRA*, London, 2003

Morton, Peter, *Emergency Tour: 3 Para in South Armagh*, Wellingborough, 1989

Murray, Raymond, *The SAS in Ireland*, Cork, 2004

Neumann, Peter R., *Britain's Long War: British Strategy in the Northern Ireland Conflict, 1969–98*, Basingstoke, 2003

O'Dochartaigh, Niall, *From Civil Rights to Armalites: Derry and the Birth of the Irish Troubles*, Cork, 1997

O'Doherty, Malachi, *The Trouble with Guns: Republican Strategy and the Provisional IRA*, Belfast, 1998

O'Doherty, Malachi, *The Telling Year: Belfast 1972*, Dublin, 2007

O'Doherty, Malachi, *The Year of Chaos: Northern Ireland on the Brink of Civil War, 1971–72*, London, 2022

O'Kane, Eamonn, *The Northern Ireland Peace Process: From Armed Conflict to Brexit*, Manchester, 2021

Oppenheimer, A. R., *IRA: The Bombs and the Bullets – A History of Deadly Ingenuity*, Dublin, 2009

Patterson, Henry, *Ireland since 1939: The Persistence of Conflict*, Dublin, 2006

Portinari, Frank, *Left-Right-Loyalist: From One Extreme to Another*, London, 2016

Potter, John, *A Testimony to Courage: The Regimental History of the Ulster Defence Regiment*, Barnsley, 2001

Powell, Jonathan, *Great Hatred, Little Room: Making Peace in Northern Ireland*, London, 2008

Purdie, Bob, *Politics in the Streets: The Origins of the Civil Rights Movement in Northern Ireland*, Belfast, 1990

Rennie, James, *The Operators: Inside 14 Company – The Army's Top Secret Elite*, London, 1996

Ryder, Chris, *The Ulster Defence Regiment: An Instrument of Peace?*, London, 1991

Ryder, Chris, *A Special Kind of Courage: 321 EOD Squadron – Battling the Bombers*, London, 2005

Sanders, Andrew and Ian S. Wood, *Times of Troubles: Britain's War in Northern Ireland*, Edinburgh, 2012

Smith, M.L.R., *Fighting for Ireland? The Military Strategy of the Irish Republican Movement*, London, 1997

Taylor, Peter, *Provos: The IRA and Sinn Féin*, London, 1998

Taylor, Peter, *Loyalists*, London, 2000

Taylor, Peter, *Brits: The War against the IRA*, London, 2002

Urban, Mark, *Big Boys Rules: The SAS and the Struggle against the IRA*, London, 1992

Wharton, Ken M., *A Long Long War: Voices from the British Army in Northern Ireland, 1969–98*, Solihull, 2008

Wharton, Ken M., *Bullets, Bombs and Cups Of Tea: Further Voices of the British Army in Northern Ireland 1969–98*, Solihull, 2009

Wood, Ian S., *Crimes of Loyalty: A History of the UDA*, Edinburgh, 2006

Websites

Accounts of the Conflict, Ulster University, https://accounts.ulster.ac.uk/repo24/ (accessed 9 September 2022)

Conflict Archive on the Internet (CAIN), https://cain.ulster.ac.uk/ (accessed 9 September 2022)

Museum of Free Derry, https://museumoffreederry.org/ (accessed 9 September 2022)

Audio-visual sources

British Universities Film and Video Council, http://bufvc.ac.uk/ (accessed 9 September 2022)

INDEX